ABOUT GARTNER:

The making of a billion dollar IT advisory firm

by Catherine Fredman

with Gideon Gartner

Including personal remarks by Neill Brownstein, Charley Ellis, Stuart Greenfield, Nadine Asin, Brad Hirschfield, and many more.

A LEMONADE PRESS BOOK

First Edition

1 3 5 7 9 10 8 6 4 2

Published by:
Lemonade Heroes, LLC
222 Broadway, 19th Floor
New York, NY 10007
LemonadeHeroes.com

Front cover portrait by Aaron Sylvan
Back cover photo from the collection of Gideon Gartner
Extra special thanks to M. M. DeVoe, for all her help.

This book is set in the typeface Adobe Caslon Pro,
with titles in Montserrat and Montserrat Alternates.

Manufactured in the United States of America

ISBN 978-0-9914548-0-8 (trade paperback)

For Sarah

Preface

"What is the purpose of this book?" That's what Catherine Fredman, a talented and perceptive writer, asked when we first got together in April, 2012. It was a valid question then as we embarked on this project and it continues to be now, as you ponder devoting your time to reading our finished product.

I never wanted to write a conventional memoir. My family knows all about me, my story is not complete, and crowding bookshelves just to take up empty spaces has never been my goal.

Instead, my interest was to engage with the many thousands of Gartner clients worldwide, as we had so many times before, in a thought-provoking "discussion" about broad technology trends, innovation, and management issues. This book would the podium from which I would present my judgments and opinions.

Now it's over two years later, and you are holding this book in your hands. The book is indeed a forum for ideas and opinions – but it's much more. To put those ideas in context, it traces the arc of the two companies I founded – Gartner Group (now called Gartner, Inc.) and Giga Information Group: what led to their creation, how they grew and flourished, and the foundation they established for the future. And in order to explain the roots of *that* story, the book also describes my own story: how a child born almost 80 years ago in what was then called Palestine came to Brooklyn, New York, studied at the Yeshiva of Flatbush, received his B.S. and MBA from MIT, and learned to follow his instincts and curiosity (with the encouragement and active help from many friends and colleagues). This lead to a path from engineering, to Wall Street, to creating two ground-breaking and successful companies. In other words, this book is a biography of both companies and their creator.

Gartner, Inc. has flourished and grown enormously since my early years. I'm delighted to see this trend continue under the brilliant direction of Gene Hall, Chief Executive Officer and a director since August 2004. Thanks to his leadership, the firm has consistently posted double-digit growth.

Indeed, Gartner, Inc. is one of the top influential voices in technology today, pushing through market hype with independent and unbiased analysis to help the world's most successful IT and business leaders make critical strategic and investment decisions. Today, Gartner insights and actionable guidance support key technology choices for 65 percent of Fortune 1000 and 80 percent of Fortune Global 500 companies.

The above alone is reason to be proud. But most of all, Gartner's idiosyncratic culture – the secret of its success – has been safeguarded by its leaders and continues to this day. My life and career have vouchsafed me many unexpected and deeply appreciated gifts, and that, perhaps, the greatest reward of all.

I expect you'll enjoy this book, but more, I hope it galvanizes your thoughts and opinions. I look forward to hearing them, and continuing the conversation.

— *Gideon Gartner, 2014*

Gideon Gartner Papers to Charles Babbage Institute

*From the Spring 2011 Charles Babbage
Institute Newsletter (Volume 33, No. 1)*

Scholarship seeking to understand the history of industries that
constitute the "information age" face some of the same questions
that companies did at the time: How large is the industry? What
are its boundaries? What are the trends shaping its evolution?
Reports from well-placed consulting and advisory companies
assessing an industry as well as appraising the trends were
invaluable to managers, executives, and investors at the time. These
reports are proving equally insightful for historians today.

For example, CBI associate director Jeffrey Yost is using the
Diebold Group reports to help chart the emergence of the
computer services industry, sharing his early research in a paper
presented at the 2011 Business History Conference (reported in
this newsletter).

We are very pleased to announce Gideon Gartner's recent donation
to CBI of a unique set of archival materials. He is well known
throughout the information technology world as founder of the
legendary Gartner Group and also, more recently, as founder of
Giga Information Group.

The archival collection — we have literally just opened the boxes — contains analyst reports from both these groups. Surely, this will be a major collection to be used for decades to come.

Gideon Gartner was well prepared to take a novel view of the emerging world of information technology. After collecting two degrees from MIT (mechanical engineering in 1956, and Sloan School of Management in 1960), he worked for IBM for several years watching its competition and then for the Oppenheimer Group watching IBM. With venture capital support he founded Gartner Group in 1979.

There Gartner developed a distinctive research process, synthesizing data, analysis, and insights into one-page reports that were sold to his banner list of clients — IT producers, IT users, and the investment community.

At Giga Information Group, founded in 1995, Gartner permitted reports to be two pages in length. On his blog (gideongartner.com) he is telling the stories of his remarkable career. CBI is pleased and proud to be the archival home for these unique materials. As soon as we can, we will make them accessible to the research community.

— *Thomas J. Misa*

Contents

Chronology

1935   Gideon is born in Tel Aviv, Palestine (now Tel Aviv, Israel), on March 13.

1937   Gideon's family moves to the United States and settles in Brooklyn, NY.

1956   Gideon graduates from Massachusetts Institute of Technology (MIT) with a BS in Mechanical Engineering.

1960   Gideon earns a Masters in Business Administration from the MIT Sloan School of Management.

1961   Gideon gets a job at Philco Corp. and moves to Israel.

1962   Gideon becomes a 'systems engineer' for IBM's 'Region 7' and thus moves to Paris.

1962   Gideon returns to Israel this time as IBM's 'Systems Engineering Manager'.

1964   Gideon returns to the United States to work in IBM's Commercial Analysis Department.

1969   Gideon leaves IBM and joins a new company called Computer Opportunities.

1970   Gideon becomes a securities analyst at E. F. Hutton.

1972   Gideon joins Oppenheimer & Co.

1977   Gideon has a life-changing conversation with Neill Brownstein

1979   Gartner Group is founded in September by Gideon.

1980   Gartner Group posts annual revenues of over $600,000.

1981   Annual revenues more than double to $1.6 million.

1983   IBM sues Gartner Group. The case is settled out of court.

1983   Annual revenues top $5.8 million.

1986   Gartner Group goes public.

1987   Gartner Group is listed #1 in profitability and #9 best small company overall in America by *BusinessWeek*.

1988   Gartner Group is sold to Saatchi & Saatchi for $90.3 million.

1990   Gideon leads a successful leveraged buyout of the firm.

1995   Gideon founds Giga Information Group.

1998   Giga goes public.

2003   Giga is sold to Forrester Research.

Introduction

The American Electronics Association (AEA) conference is an annual, high-profile networking forum in Monterey, California, where CEOs of technology companies have the opportunity to meet with small groups of powerful security analysts, bankers and venture capitalists. At this high-stakes event, top executives present, discuss, and seek funding for ongoing operations and future prospects, and traditionally, the first evening at AEA is given over to fancy private bashes hosted by the technology firms to wine and dine their top institutional investors.

On this particular lazy October night in 1977, there were two powerful men who had not gone to any exclusive parties. They ditched the noisy open bars they had been expected to attend, and instead repaired to one of the cozy seafood joints on Monterey's Fisherman's Wharf. There, wine flowed freely, the food was exquisite, and palm trees rustled with warm breezes off the ocean. The two men were having such an obviously great time, that others turned heads, their lively repartee touching upon every possible subject: music, politics, charity, technology, family, religion, chess, life...! None of the other patrons could have guessed that these two anonymous colleagues were Neill Brownstein, partner at Bessemer Venture Partners (one of the country's oldest and most successful venture capital firms) and his friend, Gideon Gartner (then at Oppenheimer & Co.).

Neill Brownstein and Gideon Gartner

Institutional Investor magazine was about to rate Gideon as Wall Street's leading computer industry analyst for an astonishing seventh year in a row and when at last coffee was served, Neill asked Gideon a casual question. Gideon paused; he could laugh off the question, or he could go into the details of a business dilemma that had consumed him for years. He could see that his colleague, Neill, showed genuine curiosity, so Gideon decided to reply truthfully.

The question Neill had asked was: "So what are you up to, Gideon?" The ensuing conversation had seismic repercussions on Wall Street and beyond!

Abraham Gartner, Gideon's father, at his neon lighting store in Tel-Aviv

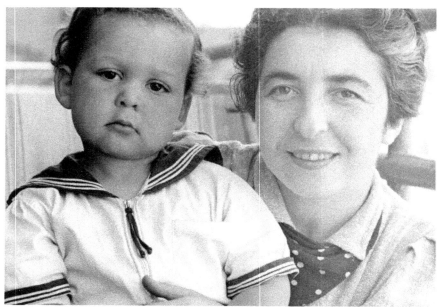

Gideon with his mother, Pnina Gartner

Chapter 1: Obstacles and Opportunities

If being a successful entrepreneur means having the confidence to stand up in front of people and persuade them to invest their time, money and resources in brilliant ideas, then Gideon Gartner didn't get off to a promising start. As a kid, he was chubby, introverted, terribly shy, and he didn't sell newspapers door-to-door or run a lemonade stand on the corner. While a good many parents today might hope their child will become the founder of the next Google, Gideon's father, a conservative-minded engineer and company lifer at Foster Wheeler (a global engineering and construction firm), would have been – and, in fact, was – horrified by the prospect of his son turning down a steady job that would pay a good pension, and as for his mother, who grew up in what was then Palestine, she did not know the meaning of the word "entrepreneur." Nonetheless, Gideon's parents instilled in him good habits and provided the opportunities that shaped his future path.

Early Home Life

Gideon was born in Tel Aviv, in what was then Palestine (1935). His parents moved to the United States when he was two and a half years old and settled in Brooklyn, New York. He grew up with conservative parents in a loving home imbued with classical music, exposure to the world at large through semi-annual vacation trips, and a strong work ethic.

Gideon's own work ethic was implanted early on when he was enrolled in what was named the 'Yeshiva of Flatbush', a Hebrew/English parochial school in Brooklyn. It has since become an Orthodox Jewish academy, but at the time it was more religiously open-minded. Having a dual curriculum led to a relatively broader education than did conventional public school, but more important, the long school hours – from 8:30 a.m. to 4:30 p.m. followed by homework – and its "no excuses accepted" policy helped develop discipline. Gideon walked to school, rain or shine, a round-trip distance of 1.6 miles.

In contrast, P.S. 217 was right across the street from the family's apartment house. Its school hours ran from 9 to 3, and Gideon was somewhat jealous of the P.S. 217 students, who at lunch and after school played stickball and basketball to work up a sweat, while he was forced to sweat over his books.

"In the short term, I would have preferred sports," he recalls. "But in the long term – class!"

When Gideon's father wasn't tending to his work as a civil engineer or chatting with friends and family, he would knock off the daunting *New York Times* Sunday crossword puzzle or settle down with a book. His favorite hobby, though, was photography. Gideon's father used to spend hours in his darkroom (closet in the apartment), often letting Gideon watch him develop and print his negatives, but Gideon somehow never caught the bug. Chess was another matter. Gideon's father taught his son the rules at a very young age, and by age 8, Gideon could think several moves ahead. His father was often too busy to play, but Gideon's neighbor, Euval Barrekette, was happy to play the opponent. Although Euval was four years older than Gideon, they were well matched, and when Gideon developed an illness at age ten that confined him to bed for several weeks, he and Euval played daily. By the time Gideon turned twelve, he could occasionally beat his own father (and seventy years later, Gideon and Euval are still close friends.)

Gideon later wrote, "One could argue that regimentation creates robotic rather than creative skills, but I'm now a big believer that students can't do well in any field without a basic foundation of good work ethics, among other values; and solid grounding was drummed into my classmates and me every day and eventually became an ingrained habit. I know many bright kids who let things slide until the last minute and rely on their smarts – and some desperate all-nighters – to get by. It works in the short term, but obviously is not a recipe for long-term success."

How does creativity blossom? In Gideon's case, through frequent Socratic dialogue with his father – at dinner, in his dad's photo darkroom, on weekend family drives from Brooklyn to Spring Valley (where his aunt ran a hotel called Gartner's Inn), during frequent chess games, or while Gideon was looking over his father's shoulder when he played bridge or pinochle. His father would ask numerous questions and expect Gideon to defend his responses with facts – nodding and adding follow-up questions when the boy stimulated an intellectual discussion. These wonderful exchanges could be on any topic – Israel and world politics, mechanics and how things worked, game strategy, religion, music – but the end result was that they left shy young Gideon with the sense that his thoughts and ideas were ultimately valuable. The more questions that were raised by his ideas, the longer the conversations, and the more proud his father seemed.

His mother was a grammar school teacher who studied piano before getting married, and she signed Gideon up for piano lessons when he was about nine. "I couldn't throw, catch or bat a baseball if my life depended on it, but piano – and later, the French horn – were things I was good at," Gideon recalls. As his piano lessons progressed, he had to face occasional gut-wrenching group recitals at his teacher's home. His teacher encouraged him to confront a piece on the very edge of his ability and practice it endlessly until his fingers could find the correct notes on their own. After weeks of struggle, Gideon would sit down to perform for his parents and fellow students. He knew that he might not mesmerize the audience with a perfect performance, but at least once he got through the piece, he could rest assured that the pressure would be off for a while. As his skills improved, he eventually grew resigned to giving recitals. Today he wonders if that pressure and preparation didn't ultimately pay off.

Gideon's parents were collectors of classical music, including opera, and Gideon loved to lie on the floor with his ears close to the stereo speakers, listening to music on 78 rpm vinyl records. Gideon played these recordings again and again, sowing the seeds for his future love of opera. "Enrico Caruso simply blew me away," Gideon recalls. "Even today, I compare those old Caruso recordings to all the greats that I followed throughout my life." Over the years, he upgraded those early 78s recordings to LPs, and then CDs, and finally bought them on electronic media.

Gideon's mom and dad also introduced him to Gilbert & Sullivan operettas, and had fun explaining the clever lyrics. Gideon's favorite was the famous patter song from "The Pirates of Penzance":

> *I am the very model of a modern major general*
> *I've information vegetable, animal, and mineral,*
> *I know the kings of England, and I quote the fights historical*
> *From Marathon to Waterloo, in order categorical;*
> *I'm very well acquainted, too, with matters mathematical,*
> *I understand equations, both the simple and quadratical,*
> *About binomial theorem I am teeming with a lot o' news,*
> *With many cheerful facts about the square of the hypotenuse...*

Music opened a new world for Gideon. The more he learned, the more he wanted to know. He developed a passion for music comparable to the passion other kids in his neighborhood had for sports. However in their sports activities, only a fraction of his contemporaries ever developed enough ability to pay dividends in later life, so in the long run, it may have been healthier for him to stay inside and practice his instruments rather than joining the street games of stickball. Music being a solo act, it was an activity at which he could race ahead at his own pace and truly excel. Music gave him his first taste of the joy of being the best at something. Gideon holds that it was the fact that his parents encouraged him to cultivate his surprising musical talent, which helped him strive to greatness in everything else he did. Music teaches a person to persevere; and so Gideon learned a life lesson: With a lot of dedication and effort, if he put his mind to it, he could make anything happen.

He eventually even picked up sports, from ping pong to stickball to softball to tennis - a sport he pursued for decades! The lesson his parents wanted him to learn was that hard work would ultimately lead to success. Music led the way.

"I was lucky to be blessed with cultured parents," Gideon says. "The U.S. shares deep cultural roots with other countries, but I sense that too many American families today are overwhelmed by superficiality: too many electronic games, web twittering and other Internet interactions, too much empty TV and low-grade movies creating overwhelming distraction which crowds out other more useful activities. It should be incumbent upon parents to force a more balanced mix of activities which will be preconditions for kids to develop disciplined habits of thought plus the skills that are necessary to succeed in business and life."

Culture Shock

Gideon attended Midwood High School, which ranked among New York City's top public high schools. Though known for being overcrowded, with extremely long hours, the school's traditional and highly structured tone was balanced by the cheerful, H-shaped building with its pretty cupola. School was, after all, supposed to be a place of intense learning. Students from Midwood High School were expected to excel, and Gideon fit right in, joining his new classmates in their obsessions with grade-point average and extracurriculars. He loved being at a "brainiac" school: with his broad interests and intense curiosity, he was delighted to meet other students who worked so hard they rarely stopped for meals. Gideon was happy. He felt at home. However, just before Gideon's junior year, his father was transferred to London.

Once a suitable rental house was found — in the Swiss Cottage neighborhood — the rest of the family moved overseas. Within weeks, Gideon had been enrolled in the boys-only St. Marylebone Grammar School, the only school his parents could find which would accept him at the last minute.

What a culture shock! St. Marylebone was Catholic. It proudly enshrined over 150 years of traditions foreign to Gideon. Each day began with the headmaster's greeting, followed by morning prayers and "comments" which included invitations for specific students to visit the headmaster's office during the mid-morning break. These visits usually involved corporal punishment, common in London schools (at least, in the Catholic ones), that took the form of formal hand-smacking and bottom-whacking from the headmaster's rattan cane, which he carried in a sheath sewn into his long black academic gown. Other teachers used whatever instruments were at hand. Gideon's homeroom master was the school's art teacher; it seemed hardly surprising that he reached for the art room's T-square to thump a hand or the backside of any boy who was not paying full attention to the lecture.

Gideon was only the second Jewish kid in the entire school. Several of the students peered at him as if he came from Mars. He was also the only American student. In 1951, England was still suffering post-war austerity; rationing of clothing, soap, and treats such as dried fruit and chocolate biscuits had only just ended, and it would be another few years before restrictions were finally lifted on meat, sugar and tea. With their country bombed and nearly bankrupted by World War II, the British attitude towards Americans tended to be either jealousy or antipathy. They felt Americans took too much credit for the Allied victories, while Britain had suffered a greater number of casualties. Gideon recalled that as a Jewish-American kid from New York, the bad vibes surging in his direction were practically palpable.

Then there was the British curriculum, an entirely different educational structure from what he had experienced in America. In the U.S., geometry, algebra and trigonometry were taught in sequence while in the U.K., these same three subjects were presented *in parallel*. Gideon was way ahead of his classmates in some cases but woefully behind in others.

Gideon continued with his piano lessons, but his new teacher was a German disciplinarian, extremely stern and demanding. In response to the pressure of having all eyes on him, both in school and out, he developed a stutter so bad that he could not even participate in class discussions. His parents took him to a psychologist who tried to correct his stutter by using flash cards; this helped a little, but didn't improve the overall situation. Gideon was overwhelmed by the changes and he suffered for them.

Nevertheless, there were many bright spots: the adventure of exploring a foreign land on weekend outings and longer vacations with his parents, attending his first live operas (*Il Trovatore, Aida* and *La Forza del Destino*), and being recruited to play French horn in the London School Symphony Orchestra. (In 2011, Gideon was surprised to receive a letter from England inviting him to a reunion of this orchestra. It surprised him to discover that he had been part of the inaugural class of an all-star ensemble that was still going strong, fifty-six years later!)

The family returned to the United States after 18 months. Gideon's stutter had disappeared, thanks to the flash card exercises of his London psychologist, although it briefly recurred at the beginning of his senior year at Midwood High School. Once again, he was the center of attention – in this case, because of his British adventures. This time, though, what made him different was celebrated rather than criticized. Some classmates chortled at his imitation of an upper-crust British accent; others saw him as a kind of hero for having survived the headmaster's cane.

Despite the brief reoccurrence of his stutter, the fact was that Gideon's confidence had picked up dramatically. He joined Midwood's chess team, sang baritone in its chorus, and played first French horn in its orchestra. Best of all, he was accepted to play assistant fourth horn with the Brooklyn Symphony Orchestra, conducted by the famous maestro Milton Katims. Katims was first violist of the prestigious NBC Symphony Orchestra and assistant to its famous conductor, Arturo Toscannini. He would become the music director of the Seattle Symphony, a post he would hold over the next 22 years, as well as accepting guest conductor honors at the New York Philharmonic, the Philadelphia Orchestra, the Boston Symphony Orchestra, the London Philharmonic and many others. "I don't know why the Brooklyn Symphony invited me," Gideon said. "I assumed it was because Mr. Chancy, the head of the Midwood music department, recommended me."

Mr. Chancy also suggested that Gideon apply to University of Miami in Florida, where he could continue his music studies with a virtual guarantee of a scholarship. But Gideon had bigger dreams. He chose to apply to Columbia, Cornell, and the Massachusetts Institute of Technology. He was accepted to all three, and immediately sent regrets to Columbia and Cornell. In the fall, he'd be going to MIT, the school he felt would be the most challenging. Thus Gideon began to embark on risky propositions that, when embraced and conquered, would eventually lead him to great rewards.

Make It Happen

Gideon developed the fortitude to move strongly ahead in life by overcoming obstacles in his path through perseverance. Most young people face obstacles. Having the stubbornness to beat these challenges builds confidence – and confidence is a common attribute of successful entrepreneurs. Successful entrepreneurs rely on many characteristic behaviors that flow from a wellspring of confidence and stubbornness: confidence hones one's antenna so as to spot opportunities and pounce on them, while stubbornness is essential to keep one moving forward, generating the ingenuity to circumvent inevitable roadblocks. In the successful entrepreneur, confidence and stubbornness ultimately transform into strength and determination.

Is it possible to acquire confidence where there is no seed? If people see themselves as mild-mannered or meek, how can they convert such traits into successful entrepreneurial characteristics?

Many people possess levels of inertia which lock them into their past. When Gideon was growing up, there were no indications that he had any characteristics of a businessman, let alone an entrepreneur. As it turns out, such characteristics can be developed. The earlier one acts entrepreneurially, whether through outside influences or innate aggressiveness, the more likely such acquired talent can be applied to greater success at home, at work, or even in one's own innovative business.

Gideon often counsels young people to dive right in to situations and projects that are challenging—embrace them! If you aren't born with it, make it happen. Find a mentor to monitor your progress and nurture positive response. Gideon wasn't born with a clear entrepreneurial bent. He didn't sell cookies on the corner or hawk lawn-mowing services around the neighborhood, but as a kid he certainly worked hard at his music with the important encouragement of his parents. He wasn't good at public speaking. He wasn't good at competitive sports. This didn't matter to his parents – they found other ways to challenge and support him. The obvious goal for anyone who wants to start a company – or anyone raising a child they hope will grow up to be the next Gideon Gartner! - is to develop confidence as early as possible and spread out over multiple and different activities, so that failure in one area does not crowd out possible success in others.

Gideon's father, Abraham Gartner

Photographed on board
R.M.S. "QUEEN ELIZABETH"

Abraham Gartner; Don Gartner (Gideon's brother); and Gideon

13

Gideon competing in a chess tournament

Chapter 2: A Complete Education

"Look at the person on your left. Look at the person on your right. One of you will not be here at graduation."

That's how the members of the incoming Class of 1956 were welcomed to Massachusetts Institute of Technology. And, in fact, the prognostication was spot on: Out of some 900 freshmen, only about 600 survived to graduate.

Few people enjoyed their undergraduate experience at MIT. In a survey conducted in 1966, most graduates compared their experience to raw combat. As one of the top teaching hubs for science and technology, the institute prided itself on being more selective than Harvard and far tougher. MIT students may not have had the social connections of their Harvard counterparts so close down "Mass Ave" but they had the smarts: nearly twice as many Nobel laureates have graduated from MIT as from Harvard. As for toughness, one senior described the experience "a battle all the way through… I was able to fight and I raked my brain to the bone, but you might have seen your buddy shot to pieces."[1]

One reason the MIT experience was so grueling was, ironically, due to World War II combat veterans. Thanks to the GI Bill, universities across the country were flooded with veterans, some

---

[1] "Unwritten Rules," *Technology Review*, May/June 2012.

eager to obtain the college degree they could never have afforded and some just happy to be subsidized to sit in a classroom while figuring out what to do next. As a result, MIT made the decision to have all courses graded on a curve, with C as the median of a bell-shaped curve. It was such a steep curve when Gideon was there, recalled Gideon's classmate Joe Rosenshein, that the median grade was 40 out of 100. "Generally no one scored 100 – and this was in a class with a group of people, many of whom were valedictorians in their high school. These were students used to being at the top of their class, but now they were competing for their lives and getting a 40. You can imagine what it did to people's self-esteem."

Life in the Pressure Cooker

After a full day of classes and lab work, Gideon and his classmates would start studying after supper and continue until very late at night. Saturday might offer something of a break, with only half a day of studying. Then it was full-on dawn-to-dusk cramming on Sunday. One student who participated in an "epidemiology of strain" survey run by the head of MIT's health service confessed that he slept with his textbooks under his pillow in hopes that the knowledge would seep through by osmosis. "Everyone was in a state of constant anxiety," Rosenshein remembered.

Gideon decided to major in Mechanical Engineering. "I did not have the background or smarts for electrical engineering or physics," he said. "I questioned my math abilities." He hoped mechanical engineering would be similar enough to his father's civil engineering career to be relatively accessible.

Mechanical engineering wasn't easy, though, and despite his enjoyment and skill at playing the French horn, Gideon quit the MIT orchestra after his first year due to academic pressures. "I was so pressured and backlogged academically that I felt I had to come up with ways to save time. I actually experimented with my sleep habits in order to reduce the number of hours required per night. At one point, I woke myself up at 3 a.m. each morning to do homework for one quiet hour, followed by a bit more sleep, thus surviving on less than six hours of sleep." That lasted one month. More successful were his time-saving experiments in personal hygiene, as a result of which he figured out how to fast-shave in twelve short strokes and shower in ten seconds.

All of this might have been worth it had his classes been inspiring or exciting, but they weren't. "I was bored to tears by most of my engineering courses," Gideon recalled.

While Gideon was lucky to be exposed to a few great teachers, exemplified by the great mathematician and founder of cybernetics Norbert Weiner *deigning* to teach a freshman calculus course, other courses for the most part were modeled on the traditional lecture/ seminar format: The professor gave erudite lectures while his graduate students attempted to explain what he was talking about in related seminars. Unfortunately, too many professors were more interested in their own research than with motivating the crowd in

MIT's lecture halls and tended to focus their presentation toward those already in the know. In those days before overhead projectors, let alone PowerPoint, the lecturer wrote findings on sliding banks of chalkboards, stacked three deep. It wasn't uncommon for a professor on a tear to cover one chalkboard with wild scribbles, then send it whizzing away on its track while he covered the next chalkboard … and the next … as students frantically tried to keep up. By the end of a lecture, the walls of the lecture hall would often be literally paneled with chalkboards crammed with equations and diagrams in no particular order.

Guidance was minimal. Photocopiers hadn't been invented, so there was no easy way for a professor to duplicate his notes. It was up to the students to attempt to decipher an arcane language that only the professor and a few chosen graduate students could speak. Gideon considered his friend Joe Rosenshein a genius. However, Rosenshein recalls, "I always felt inferior. I had a continuous feeling that everyone else was much smarter and doing better than I was. I never felt adequate."

Only one undergraduate course Gideon took sparked his innovative thinking. It was called "Creativity" and no one who took it forgot it. The class was likely designed to push students beyond the framework of standard thinking. On the first day, the professor handed out a 300-page manual describing a fictitious planet named Arcturus IV, somewhat similar to earth but possessing much different physical characteristics, such as a different gravitational pull, soil and atmosphere, all of which altered the nature of its inhabitants. The task was to imagine life on Arcturus IV and then design clothing, furniture, farm implements, playgrounds, etc. for Arcturian inhabitants, all the while adhering to the specific set of physical laws detailed in the course manual.

"The course was clearly designed to push us beyond the framework of standard thinking," Gideon recalled. "Creating our designs was fun, especially when compared with the drudgery of other mechanical engineering courses. Creativity took precedence over accepted beliefs, and going out on a limb seemed invariably more attractive than security."

Though memorable and priceless, such academic jewels were unfortunately few and far between. Not surprisingly, Gideon disliked his undergraduate academic experience. Outside of the classroom, though, he was beginning to discover a very enticing world – and to develop into a very different person.

Blowing Off Steam

Intense competition and relentless anxiety made MIT seem like a pressure cooker. But despite the stereotypical image of an engineering nerd with a pocket stuffed with slide rules and mechanical pencils, MIT was actually a wild school. To blow off steam, students engaged in pranks – which they called "hacks" – the crazier and more flamboyant, the better. Gideon, who was raised in a very strict household, was stunned that these outrageous pranks were not only tolerated, but seemingly condoned by the school's administration. Students known as "hackers" thrived on practical jokes that demonstrated technical aptitude and cleverness, with each generation striving to outdo the previous generation and "to go where no man has gone before." Hacking was so famous – and infamous – that books chronicle its history and memorialize outstanding hacks: MIT itself published a book called *The Journal of the Institute for Hacks, Tomfoolery & Pranks at MIT;* another book is *Nightwork: A History of Hacks and Pranks at MIT.*

While Gideon was a student, gunpowder was readily manufactured on campus (MIT was full of chemistry majors), and the cartridges of carbon dioxide used to add fizz to a bottle of seltzer were easily obtained. On more than one occasion the CO_2 cartridges were filled with gunpowder to make a rocket, then shot down the hallway of a dormitory. Sometimes it would explode along the way, splattering shrapnel every which way. Students such as Gideon learned the proper response to this alarming prank was simply to keep their doors closed.

This tolerance and tacit encouragement for chaos impressed Gideon to no end. How did people function in such a crazy environment, where they never knew what might hit them? The effect on the previously sheltered boy was to exhilarate him; to open his mind to the unthought-of possibilities the world could offer.

If it didn't kill you, it made you stronger. Or at least it made you laugh.

Any prank could invite another prank, especially in Baker House, where Gideon lived during his senior year. Designed by Finnish architect Alvar Aalto, Baker House is a sinuous multi-story structure made of red brick, inside and out; at the time, it was the MIT's newest dorm and its most beautiful. Some of the rooms had entrances that were inset into little alcoves, an all-but-irresistible challenge to merry pranksters. Ever resourceful, they found bricks that matched the interior walls and in the middle of the night, very quietly blocked off the doorway of the targeted room. Of course, a prank wasn't successful if it wasn't done well, so when the student inside opened his door the next morning, he'd be confronted by a solid brick wall, right down to the hardened mortar. Evil-minded electrical engineers would have already removed the mouthpiece from the room's intercom, so the imprisoned student couldn't call for help. To be sure, the window offered an escape route, but not surprisingly, this prank usually targeted students who lived on the fifth or sixth floor.

The most infamous pranksters were known as the Jolly Boys, a wild gang of mad junior scientists dedicated to sowing anarchy. Under the guise of finding unusual solutions to technical problems, the Jolly Boys hoisted everything from Cadillacs to cattle onto the top of MIT's Great Dome and even welded metal testicles to the statue of John Harvard in Harvard Square.

Rubber tubes offered irresistible options for practical jokes. Students would buy yards of the tubing used to connect Bunsen burners with gas lines, tie knots in one end and pump water into the other until the tubing blew up like a balloon. In a water fight, the pressure would blast water like a fire hose, knocking down anyone who came too close. From Bunsen burner tubing, it was a natural step to progress to inner tubes. Screwed into the window frame, they made a perfect slingshot. In one instance, pranksters catapulted a couch out of their window onto Memorial Drive.

Some students moved their pranks from their Cambridge campus to downtown Boston. One dressed up as a traffic cop, walked to the center of a busy intersection, and directed cars into an enormous traffic jam – after which, he simply left.

Although Gideon claimed he wasn't in the same league as the Jolly Boys, he said, "I learned a lot about innovation from these guys." He had loosened up enough to develop a sense of humor and participate in quieter pranks. One time during his junior year, he created a series of music tapes upon which he recorded continuous sounds of belching and dogs barking. As a music lover, he owned a pair of large speakers, which he placed in the window – then blasted the burps and barks across East Campus.

Early Experiences in Entrepreneurism

Gideon also began to expand his horizons and to experiment with entrepreneurial ventures. These included starting a sandwich business out of his dorm room on East Campus. His food source was the Harvard Square take-out shop called Elsie's, which made the best roast beef sandwiches in the neighborhood. He worked with a Swiss classmate and friend to obtain the U.S. distribution rights to a diary system called the "Seven Star Diary," which had near 100 percent penetration in its Netherlands home base, somewhat less in Great Britain, but next to nothing in the U.S. Though this business did not succeed, later other firms licensed its characteristics.

Gideon next designed and built a product he called "Solo Chess." Its general concept was inspired by the combination of an instructional device for the card game bridge called "Auto Bridge" and a monthly column in *Chess Review* in which the reader was asked to guess each next move and then graded on his logic. Gideon's "invention" was an aluminum device he had fabricated which held a series of pages that would facilitate the chess player's improvement. It was intriguing enough that chess grandmaster and eight-time U.S. Chess champion Sammy Reshevsky agreed to lend his name to the project.

While all these efforts were great concepts, none of these early entrepreneurial ideas came to full fruition. Gideon explained, "My insane MIT workload left me with no extra time, bandwidth or energy to properly follow through." But he had developed the habit of spotting potential new business opportunities and acting on them, and as a result was gaining confidence every day.

As the shy, stammering youth slowly became a distant memory, Gideon also started to ease up – just a little – on the constant grind of studying, allowing himself to have some fun. He had left the

MIT Orchestra due to time constraints, but he continued to love classical music and opera—and, inspired by the pranking on his campus, thought: Why shouldn't I take a risk or two as well? One day, when New York's Metropolitan Opera was in town – it toured regularly in those days – he made the decision that nothing would stop him from going, not even the lack of a ticket. For one sold-out performance of "Tosca," he convinced Joe Rosenshein to climb the fire escape at the theater. The two young men snuck in and mingled with the crowd in the standing room section at the back of the house. It was Joe's first exposure to opera and it turned him into a lifelong fan.

Almost every Thursday evening during the Boston Symphony's season, Gideon attended its free dress rehearsals, often inviting friends. Gideon would arrive early to be among the first when the doors opened in order to rush in to grab the best seats – "first balcony, first row, right above the stage," he recalled. Occasionally, he bought tickets for regular performances — the cheapest possible — but he was quick to seize the opportunity to upgrade, even if it required bluffing. One time, from a seat high in the balcony, he spotted an empty seat in the front row of the orchestra. At intermission, he dashed down to grab it, only to discover that a gentleman was just sitting down. He remembered his moment of chutzpah, "I guessed he had the same idea as I did, so I took a chance and asked to see his ticket, whereupon he quickly departed."

Gideon brought his determination to indulge in new experiences home to Brooklyn, vigorously seeking out part-time jobs, some unconventional. He even worked out a way to get on the Metropolitan Opera roster during term breaks as an occasional "super" (short for "supernumerary," the official name for the non-singers who fill out crowd scenes on an operatic stage). "I'll never forget standing right next to the great bass-baritone George London singing the role of Amonasro in the second act of Verdi's *Aida*," he said. It was a tribute to Gideon's newfound self-confidence that he as a non-actor and non-singer was able to talk his way onto this coveted professional stage!

Gideon never went as far as his MIT friends, however. He was appalled when, one summer, his classmate Lloyd Breslau, who had also gone to high school with Gideon, pulled a prank at Ebbets Field. Gideon and his old friend had put aside their MIT pedigrees that summer to get jobs at the home of their beloved Brooklyn Dodgers. Experienced regulars got to sell beer and hot dogs, which were priced rather high and therefore produced more tips, while newbies like Gideon and Lloyd were assigned the cheaper ice cream, peanuts, and orange drink. The drink was sold from a large and heavy tank strapped on their backs with a spigot up front. One sweltering afternoon, Lloyd suffered the complaints of a Dodger fan who loudly proclaimed, "This orange drink tastes like piss." A certified MIT prankster, Lloyd went to the bathroom, and returned boasting to Gideon that he had actually urinated in his tank of orange drink, which he then went on to sell saying that obviously, no one would ever know the difference. Gideon was shocked; he could never get his head around such a horrible prank — it was his first experience with how far some people would push the envelope. It was dreadful, but also terribly brave. The more he thought about it the more he realized that for some people, there were truly no limits — and to get away with something that immoral! It was both an outrage and a jaw-dropping achievement. He wrestled with the implications for weeks. Of course, he never knew for sure what really happened — at this point, looking back, Gideon wonders if the actual "hack" had been to get a naïve classmate to believe that anyone would actually pull such a terrible trick!

Even while he was learning to have fun, Gideon still had to buckle down and cram hard, even during summer break, both to fulfill his father's expectations and not to embarrass himself. The hard work paid off - he successfully obtained his BS in Mechanical Engineering with a respectable 3.65 cumulative average – although, he explained, "at MIT, the 'cum' is divided by 5, not 4, so I was between B and B minus." Still, despite the dean's dire predictions four years earlier and his own misgivings, he had survived the MIT undergraduate gauntlet and graduated.

In addition to his degree, although he didn't know it at the time, Gideon had acquired traits that would lay the groundwork for his future success as an entrepreneur. The demands he had faced, the people with whom he had rubbed shoulders, the broad range of experiences he had sampled – all of these fueled his curiosity, encouraged his creativity, and instilled in him the confidence to experiment, expecting that either through smarts, sheer perseverance or a combination of the two, he would come up with solutions that would allow him to meet any challenge.

Jeffrey Bolton and Gideon

28

Chapter 3: Learning on the Job

Like many college graduates, Gideon had no idea what he wanted to do with his newly minted MIT degree. Remaining idle was obviously not an option. Like many other recent grads, he looked back at his previous work experience for inspiration.

During the second half of his junior year, Gideon had participated in MIT's co-op program, an extended externship during which students worked in the real world for the spring semester and through the summer, making up their missing academic credits by taking an extra course in the previous semester. Gideon had been accepted by Curtiss-Wright Corporation, a major designer and manufacturer of aircraft engines. "It was a technology I knew very little about," he recalled. But he did well enough that after graduation, Curtiss-Wright offered him a full-time job. Gideon's first choice had been to take a position at the California-based Burroughs Corporation, which had developed an early line of computers, but when that job had not materialized, he took the Curtiss-Wright offer, despite his lack of experience in mechanics.

One of his early assignments there was to work on a jet turbine design project. The engineers had encountered a problem: Propeller blades inside the turbine were engineered to rotate very close to the surrounding housing, and in testing, the intense heat generated by the rapid rotation of the metal blades sometimes caused them to expand and scrape the housing. Gideon consulted his father, and together, they brainstormed. His father employed the Socratic method he had used in the past, guiding Gideon to identify a material that could be glued onto the inside of the housing. As the propeller blades rotated, they would scrape the material, which would be shaved down. Neither the blades nor the housing would be damaged. A later redesign shortened the blades by a few hundredths of an inch to avoid the scraping altogether.

Despite this small triumph, Gideon was depressed. His father had seemed to make the leap so easily, whereas he had struggled with the problem. Gideon liked it when things just clicked for him. Struggling seemed to point to a terrible conclusion. "I was concerned that I wasn't cut out for an engineering career. As a freshman, I had naively picked the wrong major and never sought counseling from my advisor," he acknowledged. The daily commute from the Gartner home in Brooklyn to Curtiss-Wright's plant in New Jersey didn't help. At an hour and a half each way, a minimum of three hours of the precious 24 allotted to each day were spent just sitting and doing nothing. He was throwing away fifteen hours of every week! To waste fifteen hours, getting to and from a job he wasn't certain was even his calling: This wasn't how Gideon had imagined his life. The future looked bleak.

Then fate intervened. It happened that the director of personnel at Curtiss-Wright was also a graduate of MIT's Sloan School of Management. He and Gideon became friendly, and after two months of increasing desperation, Gideon confessed he had made a mistake by accepting the job at Curtiss-Wright. "I told him I was bored, I didn't like the work and I had made a bad decision."

Much to Gideon's astonishment, the director of personnel didn't attempt to change his mind. Instead, he made a suggestion that would catalyze Gideon's thinking and set a new course for his career. "Why don't you go back to MIT and attend Sloan?" the fellow alum asked. "After all, your 3.65 cum would be good enough, and your extra-curricular activities were attractive."

It was already mid-August and there wasn't a moment to lose. Gideon jumped into his Corvette and gunned it to Cambridge. He landed in the office of Miriam Sherbourn, the head of Sloan's admissions office, and requested that he be considered for acceptance. Miriam responded, "But you haven't applied!" Gideon persisted. Eventually Miriam said, "Gideon, it's too late to apply this year, since school starts in September. But let me think about it."

Gideon drove back home and, within a few weeks, received a letter from Miriam. She had discussed the issues with others at Sloan and they came up with a solution: While Sloan could not accept him as a student *per se*, Gideon could take two courses in each first-year semester while submitting his application. Meanwhile, he could get a part-time job. (There were several firms in the area that offered such positions to MIT grad school students.) While falling short of official acceptance, it was close enough. "Of course, I would have to formally apply and then be accepted," Gideon said.

But Miriam reassured him, "We'll see how well you do in your courses, and I expect you'll do well."

"This was one of those life-changing events," Gideon recalled. "If I hadn't had the balls to drive up to MIT, my entire life would have been different. You have to make your own breaks," he continued. "You have to put yourself in a place which presents opportunities and find ways to capture them."

A New Start

Gideon promptly quit Curtiss-Wright and returned to Cambridge, where Miriam suggested he apply for part-time work at the Watertown Arsenal, a government research laboratory just upstream on the Charles River. The arsenal had hired several MITers and Gideon was assigned to a job in the foundry. This was a hot, noisy place, with roaring furnaces and clanging machines that stamped and shaped metals into precise pieces. Adjoining the foundry was a quiet and comfortable work area. The man who ran the foundry was also an MIT graduate and became a close friend, as did two others who were also taking courses at Sloan. It was a congenial and collegial atmosphere.

Gideon completed his Sloan application and was accepted. He continued to work at the Arsenal while taking two courses per semester. Unlike his previous experience at MIT, this time he was enthralled by his classes. Between his coursework, writing his thesis, and working, it took three years to earn his MS in Management.

As Gideon was taking courses in operation research, he decided to try to apply what he was learning to real-life issues at the Arsenal. One course that stood out was "linear programming" (LP), a mathematical method of evaluating several variables to help solve complex problems. In his own scarce free time, he used the LP model to approach the challenge of finding the least costly combination of raw metals with different characteristics which, when melted together, would result as close as possible to specific steel specification. He then wrote up his approach as an article and submitted it to *Foundry*, the national industry magazine, which published it.

Gideon soon realized that linear programming could also be applied to operational procedures. For example, the Arsenal had a large fleet of trucks that delivered supplies and Gideon thought he could simplify and optimize the procedure. "I simply used what I learned at MIT about queuing theory to help monitor the daily challenge of which trucks to send, where and how to keep track of them," he recalled, "and lo and behold, it worked." Gideon had met the Watertown Arsenal managing director and as a result of his accomplishments – including several other published papers– he was soon promoted from the foundry to the Arsenal's management team. His career was taking off, and he was still in his third year of graduate school.

One of Gideon's favorite classes at MIT had been "Digital Computer Logic and Programming," which explored how Boolean algebra could be used to design and enable digital high-speed computing, and its implications for machine coding. This class was his first entry to what later became known as computer programming. Gideon said, "The topic so enthralled me that I applied and, amazingly, was accepted for a position *teaching* a modified version of the same course at the University of Massachusetts in Amherst. I even used the same text we used at MIT!"

This was Gideon's first teaching experience, and it provided as many lessons for him as for his students. "Because it was 'University of Massachusetts,' not MIT, I realized that I had to modify the course to suit such a different environment," Gideon explained. "I could not just transfer the MIT course curriculum verbatim. I had to consciously reduce the scope of the course, plus the order and speed at which I taught it."

The rewards went far beyond his title of "visiting lecturer" or his fee, which was rather low. Instead, Gideon noted, "This was my first nominal but important instance of being a change agent. Nobody asked me to teach this course. I simply contacted them and volunteered. It demanded significant time that could have been applied to my job and my continuing intense workload at MIT." By now he had learned that change agent opportunities don't just happen. You can't sit around waiting for someone to notice you. Looking back, he now recognizes what had become a rule throughout his life: "An entrepreneur smells the opportunities, even on a small scale, and pounces on them!"

Introduction to Computers

In 1955, Sloan received a brand-new IBM 704 computer, the first 704 to be shipped to any university worldwide. Gideon was fascinated. As a term project, he had to write an original and challenging program for the computer. For his topic, he chose gambling.

Gideon simulated the progressive betting of what was called the Martingale System. The program had the computer run hundreds of thousands of "plays," altering the independent variables of the length of the string of bets, the size of the initial bet, the betting progression, the house limits, and the number of bets per hour. "It was a great project and I got a great grade," Gideon said. "But I should have paid better attention to my own conclusions!"

Instead he took his findings and spent a lot of time in casinos. The idea for the paper originated from his days at Curtiss-Wright, when he occasionally took a detour from business trips to the company plant in California to visit Las Vegas. His favorite game was roulette because the odds of winning a spin were extremely close to 50/50. He played using what's known as "the Martingale System," which suggests the size of one's bet. The gambler begins by forming an arithmetic progression of numbers of increasing size, such as 1, 2, 3 or 2, 5, 8, 11 and so forth. He or she always bets the combination of the first and last number; thus the first bet of the 1, 2, 3 sequence would be 4, and the first bet of the 2, 5, 8, 11 sequence would be 13. When losing a roll, the gambler adds that roll to the string, but when winning a roll, he crosses out the two outside numbers. Therefore, with the odds of each roll, winning is just a bit under 50 percent. The gambler bets when the house limit is exceedingly high; otherwise, while the player's win would be larger, a poor streak could sink him.

Though roulette was the game with the best odds, it was a game run entirely by chance. Gideon soon came to prefer blackjack, where the skill of the player can influence the odds. "After 'optimizing' the potential results which would beef up my penurious circumstances, I subsequently spent many vacations earning spending money at blackjack at the impressive rate – to me at the time – of about $20 per hour," Gideon recalled.

But, as might be expected, Gideon's luck eventually ran out. "I found myself caught in a long string of bad bets. In those days, I didn't carry much cash with me. If I had lost the next bet, I wouldn't have been completely broke but I would have been down to the point where getting out of the hole would have been unlikely." Gideon didn't know what to do: take a chance or not? He left the table, returned to his hotel room, lay down on his bed and agonized for about an hour. Should he get out? Stay in? Then and there, he decided to quit gambling for good. "The system had worked for quite a long while but wouldn't work forever. I tried to capitalize on the almost-sure win, ignoring the fact that eventually any gambler would hit a significant losing streak. In this case, although I gambled conservatively, a losing streak hit me sooner rather than later. I should have studied my own IBM 704 term paper results more carefully!"

Gideon graduated from the Sloan School of Management in 1960. "Sloan gave me a big credential, and when you graduate from Sloan, that's important," he said. In addition to learning how to apply scientific principles to the business of management, Gideon had learned significant lessons about himself: how to spot opportunities and grab them; how to catalyze opportunities rather than wait for them to occur; and, that when you find yourself in a bad situation, try your best to improve it or cut your ties quickly. He would sharpen those views even as they shaped his career over the next decade.

Gideon in Monte Carlo

Gideon at his desk

an early "computerized" office

Chapter 4: The New World of Computers

Once again, it was time to look for a job. This time, though, was different. Gideon's prospects were broader and brighter. The exciting new world of computers and management beckoned.

Gideon accepted a job with SDC (Systems Development Corporation), an offshoot of RAND Corporation (itself an acronym for Research and Development), which developed command and control systems for the U.S. government and military. SDC is considered the world's first computer software development company. (It was later sold to Burroughs and merged with Sperry to become Unisys.)

At MIT, Gideon had joined ROTC (Reserve Officers Training Corps). His undergraduate years had bracketed the Korean War, which saw the revival of the draft calling up men between the ages of 18 ½ and 35 for approximately two years of service. "If you joined ROTC in your college years, you had to serve in the military but you came in as a second lieutenant – and there's a big difference in coming in as a second lieutenant rather than as a private," Gideon recalled. The downside, however, was that in 1960, with the United States beginning its military involvement in Vietnam, Gideon's ROTC commission made him eligible for active service.

SDC helped him dodge that literal bullet. SDS employees held Top Secret clearance from the government, which meant that despite his ROTC commission, Gideon could avoid being recruited to the military.

Gideon worked at SDC doing what he called "not particularly interesting" work in operations research for the military's Strategic Air Command Control System. He had been there for six months when SDC won a contract to develop the Defense Communications Agency Control System (DCACS), a computer system that tracked and supported communications among all of the U.S.'s military aircraft. DCACS needed staff for the project and asked Gideon if he'd like to move to Washington, D.C. to work on it.

The basic concept was similar to the truck tracking system Gideon had developed at the Watertown Arsenal. But if that fact alone weren't enough to make his ears perk up, he heard through the company grapevine of an even more exciting opportunity. SDC DCACS was actually a subcontractor to Philco Corporation and Philco's computer division had just sold the first-ever, large-scale transistorized computer, the Philco TRANSAC 2000, to the Ministry of Defense in Israel! His background made him the perfect liaison; finally he could put to use his early knowledge of Hebrew from the Yeshiva school he had attended in Brooklyn. "I thought, what a great opportunity to develop my computer skills and take advantage of my knowledge of Hebrew and my MIT management experience," he remembered. "I decided to take a shot at it."

Gideon couldn't call Philco outright, of course. He was a loyal employee of SDC, which had just given him a promotion. "I suppose I could have talked to Philco on the QT but I didn't think that was honest," he said. Instead, he asked his boss to speak to the Philco people on his behalf. His boss demurred, but promised to ask his boss if it would be appropriate for Gideon to contact Philco. After some discreet urging, the answer finally came back: "If you want to talk to Philco about a possible situation, sure." As Gideon recalled, "I wangled my way into Philco by being persistent in a friendly way."

Even with permission from high up the corporate ladder, Gideon said, "I still thought it was a tremendous long shot." But he was very facile with computers – he knew the IBM 704 very well from his master's thesis work at MIT, and was also familiar with the IBM 3211 and the Bendix LG30. And, of course, there was the fact that he spoke Hebrew – and that he had an MBA from MIT "I claimed I was a businessman with a scientific background," he noted. He was immediately hired, he got married, and he and his wife were soon on their way to Israel.

It was the start of a period in his life that was both exciting and deeply satisfying, on a professional, intellectual, and personal level.

Marketing Guy

It was now 1961, and in Israel, the TRANSAC S-2000 computer was put under the aegis of MAMRAM, the Israel Defense Forces' central computing systems unit. The people working on this world's first commercially produced large scale all transistor computer were handpicked from the military and from Israel's Intelligence Corps; many were later to seed Israel's extraordinary entrepreneurial successes in the IT space. Philco executives wanted to have their machine's huge database capacity filled up and its capabilities utilized at the maximum as soon as possible, so that the Israeli government would purchase a back-up model.

Gideon was, as he put it, "the marketing guy."

"The other members of our team knew the machine and the code. I knew Philco and the computer industry – and I was Israeli-born," he recalled. An important aspect of Gideon's job was to keep his eyes open for other sectors within the Israeli government which might be interested in utilizing the TRANSAC S-2000 to develop military, scientific, or commercial IT applications. Gideon could not get enough of the powerful machine. He studied and explored the capabilities of the computer with the aid of the Israeli programmers whenever he could, and learned more and more about the rich potential of computing. "Even while being the marketing person, I kind of became a programmer," he recalled. "All my prior experience in programming computers had been scientific, using FORTRAN. But now that we were using the

Philco computers, I learned how to program commercial computers and utilize assembly language."

Gideon positioned himself as the interface between the people who wanted to see what the computer could do and the programmers who could implement their ideas. He recalled, "Even though I was quite young and inexperienced, I became a big fish in a small pond." Because Israel is an intimate country, Gideon, as the representative of a very large firm, soon found himself in meetings with very important people in both business and government.

One of these was David Familiant, the senior sales executive of IBM Israel. "I didn't think I would be very friendly towards him," Familiant recalled of his first encounter with Gideon. "In fact, I was a little upset because he was affiliated with the site that had installed the first Philco machine in Israel while I, being an IBM executive, had lost out on that deal. But he was an attractive and charming guy, a very bright young man, and we became friends." This early friendship continues to the present day.

Gideon also became closer to his mother's relatives, who lived in Israel. One of his cousins, Lihu Veisser, was building a punch-card business; in his spare time, Gideon helped him out. Gideon's first child, his son Perry, was soon born, further strengthening Gideon's own ties with his native country.

He routinely traveled between Jerusalem and Tel Aviv in search of customers to buy time on the TRANSAC S-2000. The computer had a vast capacity. At one point, he even went to Cyprus in search of business. "It was all very adventurous," he recalled.

A lasting memory of this time still exists at the Israel Defense Forces' central computing systems unit. Gideon met a man from the Netherlands who was a designer and model-builder. After asking permission from his boss at Philco, Gideon commissioned the Dutchman to design and build a model of the TRANSAC S-2000 computer. He paid for it out of his own pocket. The model was mounted on a pedestal and protected by glass, to commemorate the first large-scale computer in Israel. "It was a gift from me and it's still there at MAMRAM," Gideon notes proudly.

The IBM Opportunity

Gideon's glory days were not to last. About seventeen months into Gideon's stint in Israel, Philco announced it wanted him to return to the U.S., to a job in the company headquarters in Willow Grove, Pennsylvania. Gideon was just one month shy of qualifying for the U.S. 18-month tax exemption period, which would have allowed him to avoid paying any taxes on the money he had earned with Philco while living in Israel. "I asked if I could please stay until the eighteen months were up," he recalled. "They said, 'No, we want you here now.' That got me really upset."

So upset, in fact, that he took time out from packing to call David Familiant and ask if there were any openings at IBM Israel. David was sympathetic but nothing was available. The family's departure date was set – "We were literally ready to leave," Gideon recalled – when one evening at about ten o'clock, the phone rang. It was David Familiant. David explained that he had a visitor: the Assistant General Manager of IBM Europe, which included Israel. The executive had told David of an opening in Paris which sounded perfectly suited to Gideon's talents. "Would you like to be a candidate?" David asked. "Drive down to my office in Tel Aviv, right now, as quickly as you can."

Gideon flung off his pajamas, threw on his clothes – his experiments in speed-dressing at MIT finally paying off – and drove off to what would prove to be his destiny.

The job opening at IBM Europe was for a systems engineer in Region 7, a geographic area that encompassed everything in Europe (and Israel) except Great Britain, France, Germany and Italy. Despite not representing France, Gideon would be based in Paris; his assignment would be to offer support to smaller countries such as Denmark, Greece, and Portugal that were beginning to build their IT capabilities. The IT field was exploding and smaller countries, which had little home-grown expertise, required much deeper support than Europe's large countries. The job would involve a great deal of travel. Was Gideon interested? In addition to the fact that IBM was the world's leading IT firm, a foreign assignment with them would have important financial implications. "It sounded terrific," Gideon recalled.

The Assistant General Manager invited Gideon to fly to Paris, where he was interviewed by the General Manager of IBM Europe and offered the job. Gideon accepted on the spot. It was now 1962.

He promptly flew back to Israel and the next day called Philco in the United States to submit his resignation. Gideon and his wife removed the address labels directing their boxes to the U.S. and waited expectantly to find out where to send them in Paris.

Then, a cable arrived from IBM Europe. (That was how international communications were handled in those days.) IBM's Human Resources department had discovered that if Gideon were hired, the company would exceed its limit on the number of the number of Americans they were allowed to employ in France. IBM was very sorry but it would have to rescind the job offer. Gideon was stunned.

"My wife took the news in stride and resumed packing our bags for return to the States, but I could not accept that kind of treatment," Gideon recalled. In fact, he was so upset that for the second time in as many weeks he made an impulsive decision. Gideon wrote back to IBM: "Dear IBM, You can't do this. I accepted your offer. I'm not living in the U.S. and now I'm without a job, and I'm stranded in Israel. It's not fair and it's not what one would expect from IBM." In effect, Gideon rejected IBM's rejection.

It was a bold gamble, born of outrage and desperation – but it worked. IBM *did* backtrack, with Gideon's IBM contact in Paris promising to find him appropriate work. After some further back-and-forth conversations, a new cable arrived from Paris holding another surprise. It told Gideon he could only be hired if he joined as a European, not an American. Although he was a citizen of the U.S, he had been living in Israel long enough that IBM could sidestep regulations by assuming Israeli citizenship. It meant a significant drop in compensation, but if he accepted these terms, Gideon would be able to join one of the world's most impressive organizations in a reasonably important role. Gideon noted, "Looking back, that was amazing. I tip my hat to IBM that it went to that extreme."

Once again, the boxes were re-labeled, and this time the labels stayed on. The Gartners went to Paris. They found an apartment just outside of the city and Gideon bought a Peugeot for his 35-minute commute to the head office. Not that he was there all that often: while he had been told that he'd be making frequent business trips to the secondary European countries, his actual schedule gave new meaning to the word "frequent." IBM offices in the smaller countries had very sparse staff, so Gideon and a handful of other people in Paris constituted their entire support group. He was on the road almost constantly. Gideon quickly learned IBM's product line and its management procedures. It was a wonderful period of experiencing Europe and absorbing much computer know-how.

Seven months after arriving in Paris, Gideon was called into his boss' office. His boss had some surprising news: "We'd like to promote you," he said, "but not here." IBM had reorganized its Israel operations, demoting the existing general manager and bringing in a new one from the United States. Because Gideon already had experience doing business in Israel, IBM wanted him to return as a manager. "The new guy doesn't know Hebrew so we'd like you to keep your eyes open to make sure everything goes smoothly," Gideon's boss added. "Stay in touch with us and tell us how things are going." In short, Gideon would be returning to Israel – officially as a Systems Engineering Manager and representative from IBM Europe but unofficially as a company spy. It was late 1962.

A Terrific Time

Gideon was only 28 when he accepted the role and moved back to Israel with his young family. "Frankly," he recalled with the wisdom of hindsight, "I was not qualified for my first-ever management role." But when had that stopped him? By now, the pattern was well-etched: When you spot an opportunity, pounce, and figure out the details later.

Returning to Israel was a positive experience for the whole family. "It was a terrific time," Gideon recalled. "I had people working for me. I was no longer working with the Ministry of Defense; instead, I worked with commercial accounts." This was a good way to enrich and deepen his knowledge of what regular companies wanted from IT products and services and learn to analyze how well IBM and its competitors could meet their needs. He was delighted to discover that one of his new colleagues was his old friend David Familiant.

With IBM's permission, Gideon convinced a brilliant young programmer from the UK to join the team in Israel. "David Barrett was a super programmer and a certifiable genius," Gideon recalled. "Every time a client had a problem with an IBM machine that required a software or hardware fix, I knew the guy to call. David's skills complemented mine, and having him on my team definitely helped me succeed. That's when I first learned how important it was to have outstanding lieutenants at one's side."

Gideon's professional confidence grew. He was assuming more responsibilities and enjoyed the challenges of dealing with senior people at IBM, at his clients' offices, at the offices of potential customers, and at companies in the burgeoning IT space throughout Israel. "These were wonderful experiences," he said.

His family was growing, too. The Gartners' second child, Sabrina, was born in 1963, another opportunity to celebrate and strengthen the ties with Gideon's Israeli relatives. At the same time, each local family get-together served to remind him that he had also left family back in the United States. After fifteen happy months in Israel, in late 1964, the Gartners boarded Israel's first cruise ship, the *S.S. Shalom*, to return to New York.

It had been a rich four years since he had earned his MBA. The lessons he had first learned from his experiences at Curtiss-Wright,

MIT's Sloan School, and the Watertown Arsenal had been strengthened by the challenges he had met at SDC, Philco, and IBM Europe. Without realizing it, he was developing the fundamental character traits that shape a successful entrepreneur: the perspicacity to spot opportunities, the persistence to follow through, the confidence to make the most of them, and, perhaps most important, guts, nerve, and determination. These would become his hallmarks in the years to come.

Gideon on a business trip to Bahamas

Chapter 5: Inside IBM

Gideon was now back in the United States and, once again, looking for employment with IBM. That's the way they did things at IBM: Just because you were transferred overseas on the company's dime didn't mean there was a position waiting for you. All employees returning from overseas except senior executives had to search out and apply for openings within the entire IBM corporation. Fortunately, the company was growing, and most repatriated employees expected to find an appropriate job.

Gideon was given a list of all the departments throughout the corporation that had openings. He scheduled interviews with three.

His first visit was with a group that was developing some rather complex software. Both Gideon and Stuart Greenfield, the department manager, quickly concluded that this was not a good fit. Ironically, Stu Greenfield subsequently became one of Gideon's best friends. Much later, after Gideon had left IBM and was working on Wall Street, Stu called him for advice. Gideon helped him out, and this led to Stu's becoming a senior analyst on Wall Street, and eventually starting a major venture capital firm on his own.

For the second interview, Gideon had to drive to Philadelphia to meet with the branch manager. "I wanted to go to Philadelphia like I wanted a hole in the head," he recalled. "You could say that my teeth saved me." In those days, Gideon had major dental problems, the legacy of an orthodontist who outfitted him with braces when he was a youngster and never told Gideon when and how to clean them, or when to return for a visual inspection. It turned out that over the years, Gideon's teeth were quietly rotting. When he first attended MIT, he'd had to visit the dentist every two weeks. Later, when he returned to the U.S. from Israel, the pain from a toothache was so bad that the ship had to make an emergency detour to Malaga, in southern Spain, where a dentist was waiting on the dock to treat him. A new toothache flared up before the job interview in Philadelphia, distracting him from the conversation. Gideon didn't get that job either.

The third opportunity didn't result in a hire either, but at least it offered a temporary roost. IBM's Commercial Analysis department needed help on a project and, Gideon recalled, "Since I was just treading water, they asked me if I would work with them while I was continuing my search for another IBM job." Gideon took the temporary position and did well enough to be offered a full-time job.

At IBM, Commercial Analysis was really a euphemism for competitive analysis, which translated to IBM's topnotch intelligence-gathering operation. This was the department that prepared data for all the top executives in IBM's many divisions. The data evaluated how IBM was performing against its competition. Gideon was offered a difficult choice. The department had two sections: a product group and a market group. The product group analyzed every piece of IBM's competitors' equipment as it came into the market and compared the strengths and weaknesses of this new equipment to the functions and features of IBM's own products. Basically, the product group's job was to figure out where IBM stood in terms of its hardware and software. The market group assessed what was happening in the real world: By how much was each IBM technology beating or losing to the competition? How deep and broad was its share of the market for each of its deliverables? What were the overall and specific market trends and how were competitors reacting? By distilling a dynamic and inchoate industry into cut-and-dried data, the market group was meant to produce a clear snapshot of any given slice of the market at any given time.

Gideon was offered a choice between the two. He chose the market group.

The data was supplied by IBM salesmen. (IBM's sales force was all men in those days.) As soon as any IBM salesperson any place throughout the world found himself in a competitive situation, he had to fill out a detailed form listing the name of the other company, describing the competing product and in what ways it was competitive, and predicting the outcome – would it be a full win for IBM, a partial win, or what was gently called a "doubtful situation." This raw data was crunched by IBM's mainframe computers in the Measurement Records department, a barn of a place comprising thousands of square feet, all crammed with hardware, all constantly running and spitting out the invaluable measurements that enabled people like Gideon in Commercial Analysis to calculate where they were winning, tied, or stuck in doubtful situations, and the dollars involved in each case. Commercial Analysis, in short, was the brains behind IBM's market strategy.

Gideon would spend his entire six-year stint at IBM in that department, eventually working his way up to second-level manager.

Gideon's First Killer App

Back then, IBM was a very formal place. Employees had to wear a white shirt – only white, never even light blue – and a tie. Everyone's desk held a little wooden triangular plaque that was engraved with IBM founder Tom Watson's dictum: *"Think."*

That became the buzzword, and Gideon did think – especially about how IBM's sophisticated computers amassed vast amounts of data that were transformed into accessible information. At the time, all data was distributed in dense tables, unwieldy printouts of row after row of closely spaced figures that were anything but user-friendly. Gideon was fascinated by the challenge of transforming these statistics into accessible information and actionable strategy. "These huge reports were impossible to deal with," he remembered. "If you could develop a straightforward presentation of the measurements, it would be very useful for senior managers to have such input on a regular basis."

One day, after a year or so of thrashing through these tables, Gideon was working on a project comparing IBM products to Honeywell's when he had the idea of producing the management reports in a graphic format. He asked his boss' boss, who ran the department, if he could bring in an IBM 3211, a small computer that was a precursor of the desktop PC, and attach a Calcomp plotter to it. The Calcomp plotter was one of the first devices that could produce computer graphics. Gideon summarized the massive amount of data provided by the Measurement Records department in a graphic drawing illustrating IBM's wins and losses over time, as well as other pertinent measurements. The result was like the difference between an Excel spreadsheet crammed with numbers and an easy-to-read pie chart on a PowerPoint slide – although, of course, neither Excel nor PowerPoint had been invented yet.

Then Gideon came up with an even better innovation. A piece of paper could be cumbersome. What could he print on that would be more portable?, "I would print it out on blank computer punch cards, which could be slipped into the pocket of the white dress shirts we all wore," Gideon recalled. He sent the cards to all the managers in data processing and corporate headquarters. It was the perfect test market. "I couldn't have found a better place than the Commercial Analysis department, the center of gravity of IBM's all-important marketplace measurements."

The "control cards," as they came to be called, described IBM's competitive position for every product, every industry application, and every branch office in an easy-to-read, easy-to-understand and easy-to-carry format. They were such a hit that Gideon (who by now had been promoted to Manager of Market Information) began to think that they might have commercial possibilities. The germ of an idea began to grow: Simplify sophisticated industry data and sell the analyses to executives who had the budget to invest in such applications. That idea was the original precursor of Gartner Group.

But first Gideon had other ideas to pursue at IBM. While he was interested in how IBM and its customers could use his data to develop their macro-strategies, he was also intrigued by how companies directed their day-to-day micro-operations. A recent trend was for companies to develop "war rooms." The concept had been popularized by the famous underground suite of offices in the heart of London from which Winston Churchill had directed British military strategy during World War II. Now large corporations were buying into the idea of a central location where executives could see up-to-the-minute data and make decisions immediately.

Gideon's boss allowed him to travel around the country looking at other companies' use of data in what were then called "decision rooms." Through an IBM connection, he was allowed to visit United Airlines' decision room in Chicago. It was a huge room, hung with blackboards and letterboards from floor to ceiling. Sliding ladders of the sort seen in old-fashioned libraries crisscrossed the room. Employees scampered up and down reaching to move the letters of the alphabet around on the letterboards. The blackboards listed every single United Airlines flight. People scampered up and down the ladders, chalking in late arrivals and departures, the numbers of passengers on each flight, and various other pieces of information, while managers stood around a central table and peered at the blackboards to organize global operations. It's difficult to imagine: Even in the 1970s, United Airlines, one of the largest airlines in the world, was plotting its entire fleet by hand.

After visiting a couple of other war rooms in other industries, Gideon realized that they were variations of the same theme. Surely, he thought, there must be a way to improve operations.

As soon as he returned to White Plains, he approached his boss with two propositions. IBM management should have its own internal war room; and IBM should use its advanced technologies to create and sell prototypes of an advanced war room, complete with easy-to-use, up-to-the-minute data enabling real-time response. IBM was certainly an innovator in those days and what helped make it such a great company was a policy that Gideon's boss frequently reiterated: Any employee, regardless of seniority, with an idea which his/her manager thought useful could recruit other IBMers to a small task force to develop the idea. The only caveat was that these task force members had to work on their own time, not on company time. In other words, new ideas had to be compelling enough to convince colleagues to devote their free time after work or on weekends. It was an intimidating proposition.

Gideon gathered up his nerve and asked the head of Measurements Records and a vice president of internal IT systems and operations to join his team. To his astonishment, they accepted. After several meetings, the team of three worked up a presentation for the appropriate management committee. Gideon's manager had told him that most of these presentations were delivered to a department head. But since Gideon's idea would affect the entire division, he gave his pitch to the division president, a man named Jed Wernersbach, as well as a couple of vice presidents and senior executives. "In the IBM hierarchy, normal mortals don't get up to that rarefied atmosphere," Gideon later noted.

The presentation was a stunning success. "Everybody had their mouths open over the potential of the measurements," Gideon recalled. In fact, after he gave his presentation, the VP in charge of the whole marketing group got up and said, "Gideon, that is one of the best presentations I have ever seen."

It was, in short, a memorable proposal. But nothing came of it. Gideon was frustrated and intensely disappointed. The rejection of his creative work led him to wonder if IBM was the place he should be. But no one ever left IBM, it was a place you stayed for the duration of your career.

Walking away from Big Blue

Not long after IBM turned down his idea, Gideon happened to attend a party where he met a man who owned a small company called Computer Opportunities Inc., which trained new computer programmers in two after-hours schools, one located in New York City and the other in the northern suburb of New Rochelle. The man was very interested in the graphic data analysis Gideon was producing with the IBM 3211 and the Calcomp plotter. Gideon recalls, "Little did I realize that he would take me seriously when I off-handedly mentioned that someone should start a business creating my graphics analysis model for other companies. On our second get-together, he proposed, 'Why don't we start a business?'"

Despite this being Gideon's first opportunity to run a company, he was not about to leave IBM to head up a small string of computer schools. In those days, nobody left IBM. People vied to work at IBM and once hired, generally remained there for their entire working life. "Going to work for IBM is a lot like getting married," explained J. Gerald Simmons, a former IBMer who later became a successful executive recruiter. "It may not last forever but when you start out, that's what you have in mind." Management turnover was less than half the average for other big U.S. companies even in the go-go years of the 1980s; the percentages were even smaller in the 1960s.[2] To be sure, IBM was a large organization that didn't

---

[2] "IBM Renegades: Where Are They Now?" *Success*, April 1987.

accommodate individual interests, but it had smart people, innovative ideas, and deep pockets.

Gideon's new acquaintance might be smart, but Gideon assumed he didn't have a financial safety net. So when he invited Gideon to join Computer Opportunities, Gideon's reply was: "With no money?" "Well," the man said, "I have a little bit." Gideon pressed him for specifics. "How much?" The man ultimately revealed a number Gideon felt wasn't enough to start a business.

So Gideon declined his offer and continued to try to develop his original business idea within IBM. He wanted to build new software to allow organizations to convert long and unwieldy tabular reports into graphic form, which, as he had proved in the Commercial Analysis department, had substantial value as executive summaries. His ideas continued to meet resistance at IBM.

"I loved IBM and would have been happy to stay there under the right circumstances," Gideon noted. "But IBM didn't follow up to put me in charge of activities that would develop the war rooms or my executive summaries. I didn't want to spend the rest of my life in the same department. I'd been there 7 ½ years; that was long enough."

Gideon loved the idea of getting into business on his own but had made no strides to develop his idea into something tangible. Other than the Computer Opportunities CEO, he didn't know any businesspeople that might want to recruit him. While he was well-known to other IBMers, his fame was only internal; he had never been sent to conferences on the outside where he might meet other people who might hire him or bankroll his business idea.

However, his acquaintance from Computer Opportunities continued trying to convince Gideon to break away from IBM, constantly asking, "Have you decided anything? Would you reconsider?" Gideon finally told him, "*If* we can put together a business plan which ties together both your computer schools and my idea, and *if* you go to Wall Street and find someone willing to raise enough money to fund us both, *only* then would I leave IBM." Their ultimate gentlemen's agreement stipulated that Gideon would not leave IBM until the Computer Opportunities owner was actually in registration to go public.

Gideon never thought that this would happen. To his surprise, his acquaintance called back a few weeks later with the news that he had found a small Wall Street brokerage firm that would do a Regulation A public offering. Reg A's were the smallest investment that could be made – just $300,000, which was very small potatoes for a public offering. "I didn't really want to do it," Gideon recalled. "I knew that wasn't enough money. But I had made a commitment and felt I couldn't say no." His new partner at Computer Opportunities may have been the only person completely happy with the turn of events.

His boss was certainly displeased. Dave Allen, the head of the Commercial Analysis department at IBM had a habit of taking his shoes off when he was sitting at his desk and working in his stocking feet. When Gideon told Dave he was resigning and what he planned to do, Dave grabbed a shoe and threw it against the wall. After trying in vain to persuade Gideon to change his mind, Dave announced, "Gideon, you're going to fail." Although Gideon held his boss in high regard, the prediction didn't change his mind about keeping his promise.

Gideon's father was equally upset. "When I told my father, he nearly had a heart attack," Gideon remembered. "He saw nothing but trouble ahead, and worried himself sick." But again, Gideon stood firmly by his word.

Gideon later conceded that he had been nervous. "I did it kind of impetuously, and I didn't carefully analyze all the pros and cons." It was 1969 and the economy was stagnant. But, Gideon explained, "I'd made a promise."

Little did Gideon realize that he was in the vanguard of what would soon become an exodus of IBM talent. Within a month of hurling his shoe at the wall, Dave Allen himself left IBM to become an executive at a large technology leasing company. Other notable "IBM renegades," as they came to be called, included Jesse Aweida, founder of Storage Technology Corporation, David T. Kearns, who eventually rose to be chairman of Xerox Corporation, Alan F. Shugart, founder of Seagate Technology (the world's largest independent manufacturer of disk drives and related components), and Gene M. Amdahl, founder of IBM competitor Amdahl Corporation (later bought by Fujitsu). Like Gideon, they had all been part of a remarkable group of ambitious young men who had come to IBM during the boom years of the '50s and early '60s and helped build it into a byword for innovation and success. But like Gideon, after a certain point they felt stymied. "You taste the success, the excitement, the exhilaration of always moving, and all of a sudden the company gets very big and there are fewer opportunities," Gerald Simmons recalled. "People who grow up on wanting more, more, more and all of a sudden find it's not there, will go someplace else to get it."[3]

It took guts to start a company with very little money in a gloomy economic climate. But Gideon had outgrown IBM. He may have given up Las Vegas-style gambling but the security IBM offered couldn't compete with the exhilarating opportunity to bet on his own ideas. "If I'd stayed at IBM, I wouldn't have a real career," Gideon later said. Leaving IBM gave him a future with much stronger potential.

---

[3] *Ibid.*

Chapter 6: The Way to Wall Street

In the early months of Gideon's new venture, his former boss' prediction came uncomfortably close to the mark. "Gideon, you're going to fail." The words began to haunt him as things got tough.

Gideon had joined Computer Opportunities on the understanding that he would be able to develop his novel ideas about easy-to-read graphic presentation of data while running — and being supported by — its existing business of computer schools. But in the harsh economic climate of 1969, the imperatives involved with doing the latter precluded any possibility of truly succeeding with the former. The economy continued to weaken and the stock market began to tank – taking Computer Opportunities along with it.

"Nobody was doing any public offerings," Gideon recalled. "Underwriters were walking away from deals right and left. Even our own underwriter walked away. We were left without much money. Here I'm both running this computer school conglomerate and developing my graphics business. It was so obviously a mistake to have left IBM and join this company. I didn't know what to do."

Fortuitously, Gideon bumped into Bob Davis at a party. A fellow MIT Sloan graduate and Ph.D., Bob had founded one of the early computer time-sharing companies. After Bob told Gideon about Davis Computer Systems, which housed a big mainframe computer (in this case a Xerox SDS 940) that stored databases for multiple clients who dialed in to the computer through teletype machines. Gideon admitted that his own firm, Computer Opportunities, was having troubles. To shift the subject to brighter things, he went on to tell Bob his ideas about the graphics presentation business. Bob saw the potential, there was a second meeting, and he bought the entire company with the understanding that Bob would continue to build the faithful hardware while Gideon would begin to develop the software business. Gideon's idea was saved – but only briefly. The economy continued to go south. Soon, Davis Computer Systems itself began to run into serious market problems. When the parent company finally went bankrupt, Gideon was out of a job.

However, Gideon had read the handwriting on the wall. Before Davis Computer Systems filed for Chapter 11, he had begun to look around. One company he interviewed with was Auerbach Associates, a prominent IT consulting firm in Philadelphia. This firm had been founded by Isaac Auerbach, an early advocate of computer technology, who had been instrumental in the computerization of America's ballistic missile early warning system. He had also helped develop the first real-time computer guidance system for the United States' space program, and promoted communication between different computers. Gideon was intrigued. Auerbach Associates was known for evaluating prospective hires through a series of rigorous intelligence tests, and Gideon sprang at the challenge.

He aced the tests. The summary read, in part, "Mr. Gartner is a very bright and knowledgeable manager whose education and past vocational experiences have served him well in terms of providing him with the concepts and organizational ability he is now able to put to good use....He has a quick and active mind and has little trouble arriving at decisions. He can be methodical when he has to, but he also can make critical judgments quickly without jeopardizing the overall project at hand." It was such a confidence booster that Gideon kept the test results for years. Of course, Auerbach promptly phoned and offered him a job.

It was now early 1970 and Gideon was all set to join Auerbach when, about a week after the phone call, he received another call. Out of the blue, a senior executive at one of the most respected firms on Wall Street, called Gideon to say, "We'd like to talk to you about possibly becoming a securities analyst in the technology area at E.F. Hutton."

"Why me?" Gideon asked. The story that unfolded was one of those fortuitous tales of having known the right people who resurfaced at exactly the right time and place. Back when Gideon was forming his small task force at IBM to develop the idea of creating modern war rooms, one of the members of the task force was a senior executive within the data processing division. The boss of that executive was Jed Wernersbach, the president of the entire division in charge information technology. He had been in the room when Gideon formally presented his innovative ideas to IBM's most senior management. And now the connection resurfaced: Jed Wernersbach just happened to be the next-door neighbor of one of the VPs who ran Hutton's research department.

As the Hutton executive explained, he had walked over to Wernersbach's house and asked if Jed could recommend someone at IBM who knew something about the computer industry and might want to become a Wall Street analyst. Wernersbach said, "Of course, it would be inappropriate and unethical for me to facilitate an employee of my own company jumping ship. But there's this guy with whom I worked, Gideon Gartner, who just recently left IBM. I was on his committee when he was trying to invent a war room here. He worked in the department which tracked and analyzed IBM's competitive environment, so should know the competitive space very well.'"

The grilling Gideon got at E.F. Hutton made Auerbach's tough test look like child's play. Finance pervaded Wall Street's institutional research. Except for one class in accounting and another in economics at Sloan, Gideon knew nothing about it. He didn't see how he could possibly fit in. But Hutton seemed to think otherwise. And when Gideon asked for advice from two friends who worked on Wall Street, they both said, "Go for it."

E. F. Hutton offered Gideon a job as a securities analyst, even though securities analysts on Wall Street generally had years of experience investing in stocks. Gideon had none. Despite his trepidation, he accepted and started working at Hutton in May, 1970. At the time, Wall Street didn't routinely offer the kind of big bucks it is known for now. Gideon would be starting at $25,000 per year, the same salary that he had previously earned both at Computer Opportunities and at IBM.

The job Gideon was turning down at Auerbach Consulting had offered a higher salary and would have been more in line with his experience but taking it would have been ignoring his nature. Auerbach's management psychologists had discovered a further trait in Gideon: "Mr. Gartner could be setting his overall goals a little bit higher, although this is not a serious fault. He could also be producing more in the way of innovative and original ideas; this, of course, is an area in which the need is measured by the company."

In the past decade, Wall Street had evolved from treating security analysts as back-office number-crunchers to what *Forbes* magazine dubbed "The Money Men" in "the age of analysis."[4] With the institutionalization of the stock market in the 1960s, the article explained, "Big institutions began to be run by men who [already] had access to standard information. What they needed was *extra* information, *fast* information, *exceptional* judgment. Their brokerage patronage began going to firms that could supply it. Says Leon Levy [senior partner of Oppenheimer & Co.], 'With the growth of institutional investing, we finally had customers who could pay well for detailed security analysis.' The analyst, the office

---

[4] "The Money Men." *Forbes*, July 15, 1972.

drudge, had become Mr. Big. The Age of Analysis had arrived on Wall Street."[5]

Hutton's famous slogan at the time announced: "When E. F. Hutton talks, people listen." Gideon now had his first chance to speak from a bigger pulpit and make an impact in a rapidly growing, exciting industry. He was nervous, but how could he resist?

Wall Street, Here I Come

There was no logical basis for Gideon's assumption that he would be successful on Wall Street. He didn't know *anything* about finance. But he did know computer companies. And his timing was perfect.

As luck would have it, IBM had just declared war on Xerox's copier business. Xerox had invented and practically owned the copier business, but its monopolistic pricing cracked open the door for competitors. IBM had just stepped in with its Copier 1 and the Japanese were gearing up to move into this space, too.

Gideon spoke to various contacts at IBM until he found a guy who was just beginning to sell IBM copiers; from him, Gideon was able to obtain an idea of IBM's strategy. Xerox's modus operandi with its large copiers was to sell one at a time: The machines were big and fast, but so expensive that many companies couldn't afford

---

[5] *Ibid.*

more than one per company or department. How would IBM compete? Its strategy was to sell two printers at a time. IBM's printers weren't as fast but they were cheaper, and a department with two printers could have more people working on them simultaneously, which would be more efficient overall. Gideon started to play games in his head about the impact IBM might have on Xerox, even though IBM was effectively starting from zero.

Xerox stock was one of what people then called the "Nifty Fifty" portfolio, a bunch of reliable earners that investors bought to hold in perpetuity. For Gideon's initial report to his new set of clients, he wrote the very *first* negative report on the Xerox Corporation, suggesting that Xerox might be heading into trouble and backing up his argument with data and analysis from every possible angle. "Talk about chutzpah!" he gleefully recalled. (This report can be found in Appendix A.)

The Hutton sales force went wild. Every Hutton client routinely received all analyst reports from every one of Wall Street's "sell-side" firms, but now Hutton's sales people called each "buy-side" client who might purchase stocks and asked, "Have you read Gideon Gartner's report?" The reaction was unprecedented. The clients were shocked by Gideon's report but also very interested. Hutton's salesmen set up dozens of meetings and Gideon was flown around the country to visit virtually every medium to large bank, insurance company, non-profit foundation, and investment fund that held investments in Xerox – in other words, most of the money managers and analysts of almost all of the buy-side organizations in the United States. He was on the road continuously for the next four months.

It was too early to know whether Gideon's conclusions about Xerox would prove correct, but the report immediately put the Gartner name on the map. And then, once it began to look as though his analysis and predictions were accurate, his reputation soared. At the end of his third quarter of working at Hutton, he received a bonus of $25,000 – a bonus that equalled his annual salary. Gideon ran right out and bought a blue, two-seater Mercedes 250 SL convertible. The price tag: his entire bonus.

Gideon had been carpooling from Mamaroneck, a suburb of New York City, but now he started to drive to the Hutton office on his own. He installed a dictation system in the car. Almost every evening, he'd come up with a new idea or a different analysis of some issue that he felt could and should be disseminated to Hutton's broad client base. The next morning, he'd dictate a brief message to the sales force as he drove to work. These messages became an additional excuse for Hutton's sales people to touch base with their clients. One of the sales people called Gideon's morning news snippets "sunflowers," because the sales force gobbled up his research and parroted it to their clients like parrots munching sunflower seeds. To this day, everyone who was then at Hutton remembers "Gideon's sunflowers."

Reaching the Big Leagues

Gideon worked at Hutton for only 18 months, though he was almost immediately recognized as one of the best analysts in the firm. As his reputation grew, so did recruitment calls. One of his best clients insisted, "You shouldn't be at Hutton. You should be at Oppenheimer." Along with Salomon Brothers and Goldman Sachs, Oppenheimer was known as one of the top three trading and research firms on the Street. Gideon's client introduced him to his uncle, Leo Mandrakos, who happened to be Oppenheimer's director of research. At the time, Hutton was going through an unpleasant negative dispute between the institutional research department, where Gideon was based, and the retail department, which wrote reports for all of the individual investors. Gideon explained, "In the parlance of the time – this was early 1972 – there were bad vibes in the company, and I didn't see any likely improvement. After several months of regular lunches in the partners' dining room with Leo, I was convinced to jump ship."

In hindsight, Gideon said, "I believe that knowing when to leave one's employer is a critical success factor in building a career, assuming that the logic behind one's decision makes some sense. I think every budding entrepreneur knows when to move on."

In less than two years, Gideon had reached the big leagues. Again, he asked himself: How might he make a mark competing against the awesome concentration of brainpower on Wall Street, the likes of which he'd never had to compete against before? Two Wall

Street firms, G.A. Saxton and G.S. Grumman, who were famous for large technology analyst teams of roughly eight analysts each, seemed to have a complete lock on the industry.

The solution?

Gideon said, "I had to figure out a way of being different, not just along the rather trivial lines of writing a contrarian report as I did with Xerox, but something that would cause me to be recognized as standing out."

Here's how he did it: Most Wall Street analysts who followed the computer field covered two dozen or even more companies in some detail. They focused on financial information more than industry fundamentals and spread their expertise, as the saying went, "a mile wide and an inch deep." But the Wall Street tech analysts took such a broad perspective that they missed a significant fact: IBM was not just one among a bunch of technology companies, but *the* technology company to watch. Anything IBM did would either subtly or explicitly impact the entire space. Gideon knew this as a result of his seven years of working at IBM; in fact, as a result of working in the commercial analysis department, he knew *precisely* how IBM affected the competitive environment.

Gideon put his knowledge to use and positioned himself as the the de facto expert on IBM. "This immediately elevated me to a position where investors were interested in speaking with me and in reading my work, almost regardless of what company or sector they were agonizing over," he noted. A cynic might say that IBM was the only IT firm Gideon knew anything about. This was somewhat true in the beginning, but Gideon was able to position this "flaw" as a selling point, and rapidly fill the gaps in his knowledge as he used his expert status to solidify the connections he needed to expanded his coverage base. The entrepreneurial factor was in figuring out how he could leverage his initial knowledge of how the IBM behemoth would (or would not) affect its important competition.

Differentiation from others became Gideon's modus operandi on Wall Street. When visiting with clients, most other analysts chatted across their client's desk in a very familiar manner, as if they were having a friendly interview. Remembering the success of his IBM punch cards, Gideon chose to present his pitches formally, via a three-ring binder containing charts detailing his research analyses. He'd prop the binder on the desk in such a way that the client could better follow while he leafed through his arguments. This style was simple but it set him up as both an expert and a professional, and definitely helped differentiate him in a very positive way.

Gideon's different style was backed up by substance. At the end of Gideon's first year at Oppenheimer, while he was still fresh on Wall Street and had not yet figured out the world of finance, *Institutional Investor*, the only reputable analyzer of who's best on Wall Street, rated him the Number Two technology analyst. The next year, he was ranked Number One.

But then *Institutional Investor* faced a dilemma: Some of the overlooked firms complained that the rankings were decided by calling every buy-side investor once a year and asking which individual analysts were giving them the most help. But Gideon's competition wasn't any *one* other analyst; it was *groups* of analysts. G.S. Grumman had six senior analysts covering the technology industry; G.A. Saxton had seven, and both had additional back-up teams. Gideon, as a comparison, had one chap who pushed numbers and helped with spreadsheets. Gil Kaplan, *Institutional Investor's* founder and owner, came up with an inventive solution: For each of Gideon's ensuing years at Oppenheimer, Grumman and Saxton alternated between number one and number three, with Gideon consistently ranked the number two individual technology research analyst on Wall Street. He held that honor for seven years running.

So what did Gideon learn from his roller-coaster experience between leaving IBM and finding a successful footing on Wall Street? He said:

"In hindsight, the underlying lesson was to articulate what I already instinctively knew: that *being different*, if thought out and tested sufficiently, is one major method to achieve attention – and maybe even success.

"And secondly, that if you establish positive preconditions in life, they may pay positive dividends in the future. One never knows!"

Gideon had also developed the confidence that well-considered risks weren't necessarily to be feared and avoided, but, in fact, could be rewarding. His experiences at MIT, Philco and IBM, while occasionally demanding courage, had all turned out well. The collapse of Computer Opportunities even after it had been "saved" by an acquisition was a true business failure – but even then, Gideon had remained unemployed for only a few weeks. His crisis of confidence was brief, almost immediately erased, first by Auerbach's stellar evaluation, and then by E.F. Hutton's decision to hire him.

Gideon had learned to equate risk with reward. He had confidence in his abilities, even in situations where he didn't have conventional training. But Oppenheimer was the most important Wall Street firm of the time – Gideon braced himself, expecting to be tested in a big way.

Gideon in tough negotiations, relaxed under pressure

Chapter 7: Do It Yourself Gideon

On Wall Street, Gideon prospered far beyond his expectations. He had been made a vice president at Oppenheimer, and was on the path to full partnership. His prescient calls won him top honors from the investment community. He had won the respect of his industry.

"Gartner is a creative thinker with a unique perspective on the broad technology industries," said James Yacobucci of Cumberland Associates, a well-known private investment firm. "He has the uncanny ability to take a piece of information, such as a product announcement, and accurately determine not only the impact it will have on the individual company, but also the implications for its competitors, the industry as a whole, and even related industries. Gideon is not afraid to vary from the party line and a remarkable number of his long-term forecasts have proven prophetic."

Gideon's time at IBM had certainly served him well. "I had a leg up understanding the data-entry firms, and all the many firms selling peripherals," he recalls. "I was also more active than most other analysts in organizations such as the Computer and Communications Industry Association (CCIA), and besides following all the mainframe companies such as Burroughs, Sperry Univac, Honeywell, and Control Data, and the important peripherals and software companies, I had made my clients lots of money in stocks such as Centronics Data, Data Products,

Management Assistance, Storage Technology, and mainframer Sperry Rand."

Gideon's research at Oppenheimer soon found an audience beyond the Wall Street community. In the course of his research and through association gatherings, he had established relationships with many senior executives in the computer industry. "Every time I met an executive, I asked him, 'Would you like to be on our mailing list?' Many people asked to receive my research, and Opco, as it was known on the Street, gave me the green light to send it to them."

In addition to investors and technology users, Gideon also had an impact on computer *vendors*. David Stein, who would later become a co-founder of Gartner Group, recalled that when he was in charge of developing a new computer system at Sperry Univac, he challenged his team to find out what IBM was doing in the same space – not an easy task given how closely Big Blue guarded its strategy. "To my surprise, my team got the information in detail," Stein recalled. "When I found out who they got it from, the answer turned out to be an analyst at Oppenheimer named Gideon Gartner."

But despite the acclaim he was receiving, Gideon was frustrated. Again, he had plans for a profitable new line of business — but just as had happened at IBM, Oppenheimer wouldn't let him expand.

Desperate for additional help, Gideon came up with an idea for a business within Oppenheimer that would create a revenue stream rich enough to pay for extra staff. The IT industry executives who were on Gideon's mailing list had made it clear how much they valued his insights. Knowing this, Gideon went to his senior managers and proposed that they price his research for non-Wall Street consumption and find a means of marketing it. Oppenheimer grudgingly agreed.

Gideon promptly hired two people to his team. The first was Aaron Orlansky, an ex-client who was working as a technology analyst in Paris for Sogen Swiss. He came on board; a marketer with hot insights from the European front. Orlansky agreed to commute between his base in Paris and New York, thereby keeping those European insights fresh. The second new hire, salesman Bill McAffery, was one of the founders of McAffery/Seligman/Von Simson, an organization that provided IT industry analysis to a "club" of senior executives in management information systems. McAffery already knew many of the players on Gideon's mailing list and, better yet, knew others who should be on it. His organization was later renamed The Research Board and was much later acquired by Gartner Inc.

Even with these new hires, everyone was working overtime. Gideon recalled, "I was continuing with my research responsibilities to Opco's financial clients, and Orlansky was shuttling back and forth collecting intelligence from his Parisian contacts, and McAffery was selling our content plus quarterly meetings to IT user executives. We built up to twelve clients who were each paying us about $5,000 a year, a small enough number that didn't cover the expense of our new Opco business completely but we were in the process of expanding." The market had vast potential, which Opco had recognized, but aside from the two new senior hires, the firm refused to give Gideon the freedom to really mine the opportunities. "Oppenheimer viewed our business as outside of its main stream of interests, plus it interfered with my primary responsibility of doing financial research and servicing institutional investors," Gideon explained. "It effectively limited our potential."

The Deal

When Gideon poured out his frustrations with Oppenheimer to veteran venture capitalist Neill Brownstein over dinner in Monterey on that warm October evening in 1977, Brownstein stared out over the moonlit Pacific, a bemused expression on his face. "Gideon, why don't you do it yourself?"

It was the simplest solution in the world, but Gideon hadn't until that moment considered it. He had spent the last several hours at the AEA annual conference mingling with people whose ideas were not half as good. But to start his own firm – to quit Oppenheimer? Despite his frustrations with the firm,

Oppenheimer was the most respected voice on the Street, and Gideon was now a limited partner with excellent prospects. He was on top of the heap professionally and earning exceptionally good money with even more to come should he become a full partner. Virtually all full partners on Wall Street are multi-millionaires. Quitting Oppenheimer was as crazy as the notion of leaving IBM. Crazier.

And yet ….

Gideon shared with Brownstein his secret ambition to take another crack at running a company. Furthermore, he believed his research style would beat the pants off the then-leaders in the technology market research business: International Data Corporation (IDC), DataQuest, Input, and Yankee Group. Brownstein agreed that Gideon was stupid to stay at Oppenheimer; after all, Gideon had a good idea and had already shown that he could attract external business—why not do it commercially?

If Gideon had learned one thing from his Computer Opportunities experience, it was the need for deep pockets. "I was neurotic about being under-capitalized since my first company ran out of cash during the 1969 recession," Gideon recalled.

Raising enough money to successfully get a new business off the ground was notoriously difficult. A year or so earlier, Gideon had experienced this first-hand when he had spoken with Dave Norman, founder and then-CEO of DataQuest about the possibility of joining his firm. Norman had forged an extremely successful business selling market research to vendors. The two men met while Norman was in New York, and Gideon impetuously commented that he could bring something very major to DataQuest. Norman showed interest, and Gideon described his ideas. DataQuest could sell market research information to users. After all, *this* was where the big dollars were spent and where the stakes were highest. Norman perked up but having already built a thriving business without tapping the user market, he was only mildly interested. Gideon tried to explain that the big opportunity was *not only* to sell to vendors but to users *as well*. This idea was outside of Norman's scope of vision. As it turned out, Norman was already scheming to sell DataQuest, which he succeeded in doing shortly thereafter. (He sold it to Nielsen, which itself was gobbled up by Dunn & Bradstreet several years later, and, ironically, eventually acquired by Gartner Inc. It's possible that Norman either couldn't absorb Gideon's concept or was just too busy to explore it.)

Yet now, not too long after being turned down by DataQuest, Gideon found himself sitting across a table from Brownstein, a top venture capitalist, who was encouraging him to start a firm, presumably with his own capital! Didn't would-be entrepreneurs have to spend significant time preparing detailed documentation and glossy proposals and so forth, to command VC attention? The irony of this opportunity was staggering.

Gideon knew next to nothing about how the venture capital community operated, so he asked Brownstein how a deal might be structured. Brownstein searched through his pockets and pulled out a letter he had stashed inside his jacket; on the back of the envelope, he jotted down some figures. "Here's what a deal would look like," he said.

It was that easy and straightforward. Brownstein was an innovator; he saw an opportunity and seized it.

While there were some subsequent alterations to the deal, those early scribbles proved remarkably close to the ultimate agreement. Brownstein was clearly in the driver's seat because of Gideon's inability to fund the idea himself, so there was not much room for negotiation. Gideon noted, "Regardless, I preferred to work with OPM (Other People's Money) rather than my own. And little did I know then that there was *seldom* much room for negotiation with venture capitalists."

Brownstein served on the board of directors of computer maker 4-Phase Systems with Christopher Brody, a general partner at E.M. Warburg Pincus, a major private equity firm with major investments in technology. Brownstein invited Brody to meet Gideon, so that the two VCs could listen to his pitch and consider together whether to go ahead with the deal. The result was a noteworthy meeting of the minds – and a major step toward starting a new company.

The form of the proposed deal was instructive in illustrating to Gideon the mindset and approach of venture capitalists. The VCs would capitalize the company with 6,250 shares of "two-times preferred" stock at $100 per share, of which the VCs would buy 100 percent. There would also be 100,000 shares of common stock at 50 cents per share (a total equity investment of $50,000), which would be divided three ways: one-third to the VCs; one-third to Gideon as the founder; and one-third to other management people who would join the business. Gideon's own cash investment for one-third of the equity in this new company would be only $17,000.

"Two-times preferred" stock was a term Gideon had never heard before. Essentially, it meant that not only would the preferred stock carry an 8 percent interest rate "coupon," but its face value would increase at the rate of 15 percent per year. In other words, in five years, the face value would rise from $625,000 to $1,250,000, the sum the young company would have to pay to redeem the outstanding preferred stock. If the company couldn't redeem it, the voting rights would shift dramatically in favor of the VCs, and their one-third equity position would instantly become a controlling interest in the business, enabling them to make whatever management changes they chose or, more likely, to recapitalize the firm further in their favor. All this for a relatively small investment.

"A $1.25 million potential debt burden seemed like quite a hurdle for a company with zero revenues," Gideon recalled. "Luckily for me, at the time I had no concept how difficult it would *really* be to build a business of sufficient scale to comfortably pay down this debt. Any prudent analysis of this deal might have convinced me to walk." Being naïve, he rationalized the downside by convincing himself that if things didn't work out, he could always get another great job on Wall Street.

Meanwhile, the VCs and Gideon were all too aware that he comprised a one-man show. They weren't going to fund a business with a staff of one. At least one strong partner had to sign on before the funding spigot opened. Gideon happened to know exactly whom to call.

David Stein and Gideon had first met on a project for Thomson CSF, a French peripherals company interested in buying California Computer Products (Calcomp) and looking for a comprehensive evaluation of its proposed acquisition. Gideon recalled, "Dave and I worked around the clock, interviewing virtually every ex-Calcomp employee, Calcomp suppliers, and others who had any standing to understand its prospects. We were literally up all night two nights running before we were to leave for Paris, and the actual presentation was acclaimed by the Thomson executives as the best staff work they had ever seen."

It was a bonding experience whose strengths were reaffirmed during a subsequent study for Storage Technology. "Dave was the technical genius and I was more the inferential analyst, organizing the activity and choreographing the dance which was an essential element in the project's success," Gideon explained. "Dave deferred to my judgment on all matters of project management and gave full weight to my analytic conclusions. He bought into my interview techniques, my approach toward triangulation of inputs from multiple sources, and so forth." David was a natural choice to become co-founder of Gartner Group and, in fact, he turned out to be a critical success factor during its first five years. First, however, he had to be persuaded to quit his job with a well-established firm and take a chance on a new business.

A side note: In parallel with the discussions with Neill Brownstein and Chris Brody, Gideon contacted two other very major VCs whom he knew reasonably well, Fred Adler of Adler & Co. and Gideon's close friend Stuart Greenfield of Oak Investment Partners, to see if they might wish to join the two "unnamed" VCs who were already onboard. They both declined; curiously, for the same reason: both had negative attitudes about investing in "people businesses," because they had less inherent leverage than manufacturing companies. Despite having to disappoint him, Stu Greenfield remained a close friend of Gideon's for many decades, and recalls his turndown vividly – but now he blames the decision on his partner!

Tough Choices

It was Gideon's sixth year at Oppenheimer, early 1978. His workload was unreal. His side business providing market analysis to external senior IT executives had fifteen paying clients, while he continued to provide research for Opco's institutional investors. He was polishing a detailed business plan for Brownstein and Brody, while also twisting Dave Stein's arm to persuade him to quit his job with Harris Corporation and join Gideon for ten percent of the ownership of the nascent firm. If all that weren't enough, he was also stalling Oppenheimer's president, who had chosen that moment to meet a tough demand.

"Steve Robert, Opco's president, was pushing me more aggressively than ever to sign a non-compete agreement relating to the industry-oriented business which I was building," Gideon recalled. "But he didn't offer any quid pro quo for the non-compete, which I had insisted upon from the start." Gideon had earlier agreed that cash compensation pay-outs enabled by the fees charged to the fifteen major clients of his firm-within-a-firm would go exclusively to Orlansky and McAffery. Gideon's own goal was to build staff which could add to the breadth of research he was delivering to Wall Street; that, in turn, would help him maintain his position as a top security analyst, with attendant compensation. "So while the VCs were negotiating with me, with no guarantee yet that we would come to terms, to cover my bases, I argued to Steve Robert that Oppenheimer should set up a more formal business for me and redefine my priorities. Of course, from Oppenheimer's point of view, my priorities started and stopped with servicing the institutional investor clients!"

All this took time, but the day was inexorably approaching when Gideon would have to decide whether to fish or cut bait: sign the contract with the VCs or stay at Oppenheimer. Until the very last moment, he wasn't sure what to do.

It all depended on whether Oppenheimer was willing to shift its stance on Gideon's role and let him be an in-house entrepreneur. Gideon thought there might be a good chance to compromise, which would result in some form of continuing relationship. "I knew what the pressures were within Oppenheimer to maintain the integrity of the research department as a top-level force on Wall Street," Gideon explained. "Among the twenty-five or so senior analysts, there were perhaps only five who really carried the department – not an unusual ratio on Wall Street. The sales force would not relish losing one-fifth or more of their heavy hitters and would put pressure on Oppenheimer to negotiate some deal which would maintain my contact with institutional investors at whatever level."

Gideon then consulted Dave Stein about whether he would be willing to join Gideon at Oppenheimer. There, he hit a snag: Dave was definitely not inclined to leave Harris Corporation for "just another employer," compared with being the co-founder of a new company supported by VC giants.

Feeling conflicted, Gideon chose to confide in Bruce Brandeleone, Opco's executive manager of institutional sales and a friend. Gideon said, "When I mentioned the VC negotiations, he expressed shock! He repeated his view that I was one of five heavy hitters who 'carried' the department and was therefore indispensable. Before our discussion ended, he insisted the two of us brainstorm possible deals which would encourage me to stay." Brandeleone also promised to keep their conversation confidential.

True to his promise, Gideon shared *his* dilemma with Neill Brownstein and Chris Brody. Brody's temper flared. "Wait a minute!" he stormed. "You can't expect us to go to our investment committee and obtain a funding commitment while you're still negotiating with Oppenheimer, and possibly let Oppenheimer take the business away from us." (Gideon couldn't resist thinking how ironic it was that they already considered it their business!) Although he understood Brody's point of view, Gideon could not see cutting off the option of staying with Oppenheimer, if by chance Opco could make it *really* worth his while.

Neill Brownstein broke the impasse. "Why not ask Oppenheimer directly to join us in the deal?" he suggested. "Let's make them a partner!" In other words, Opco should be asked to join Bessemer and Warburg Pincus, investing in and supporting the new company on an equal basis. Opco would then reap the returns on its small equity investment. In addition, it would have access to a much greater volume of high-quality research, which would not only benefit Opco's institutional clients, but put them in the undisputed leadership position among technology analysis on Wall Street, with a long-term franchise which might be unassailable. Brilliant! It would be a no-brainer for Opco to at least consider, and seemed to Gideon a solution it would accept.

The next day, Gideon shared Neill's new vision with Bruce Brandeleone, who immediately acknowledged its merit. The following day, Brandeleone convened a meeting with Oppenheimer's heaviest hitters: himself, Gideon, research director Bert Fingerhut and president Steve Robert.

Gideon had spent the previous evening preparing his signature flip charts. As the meeting began, he confidently presented a well-thought-out description of the huge business opportunity for a newly designed research firm, and why a creative and ambitious individual such as himself was drawn toward these "natural" market opportunities and could not in principle reject them. Gideon then described how some venture capitalists had approached him (as Neill, in fact, had), and described how, through his loyalty to Oppenheimer as a partner (albeit a junior partner), he had prevailed upon the VCs to invite Oppenheimer in as a full participant, and to agree that the capital to be invested in the new firm would actually strengthen Opco's technology research position, which would offer a significant upside. "Yes, I gilded the lily some," Gideon conceded. "But I expected my presentation to be a no-brainer opportunity for Oppenheimer, a win-win for all."

This was the first time Steve Robert had heard anything about Gideon's pending relationship with VCs, and he turned ashen. He must have felt that Gideon had blindsided him by stringing out the discussions on the non-compete issue and refusing to sign. Within a few minutes, it was obvious that he had stopped listening. When Gideon stopped talking, Steve turned to Fingerhut and asked, "Bert, did you know that Gideon was working with venture capitalists?" Fingerhut had not. Steve Robert immediately rose and stalked out of the room. The meeting was over.

Word spread quickly. Several senior Opco partners tried to convince Gideon that leaving would be a huge mistake. The Oppenheimer senior sales people were very vocal at the prospect of losing Gideon's research but even as a group they had little clout. Bruce Brandeleone tried to explain the new opportunity to Steve, but made no headway and may even have compromised his own career by taking an overt stance on such an emotional issue.

For his part, Gideon met with Jack Nash, one of Oppenheimer's two famous founders. Jack was known as a very tough guy. He listened as Gideon explained the pros and cons of the investment, but ultimately responded that this was Steve Robert's baby, and that he would not meddle. However, Jack Nash may have put his two cents in with Oppenheimer's president, because a few days later, Steve stopped by Gideon's office to offer an alternative solution.

He proposed that Gideon's small staff of Aaron Orlansky and Bill McAffery would be funded as a separate entity within Opco with an initial $100,000 line of credit. Gideon would obtain a 25 percent equity interest in the new business and he would finally become a full Oppenheimer partner. In other words, Steve was asking Gideon to drop the VCs in return for an offer that could be worth a fortune. It was very tempting – and in retrospect, Gideon mused that had Robert offered the full Opco partnership at the meeting with Brandeleone and Fingerhut, it would have cemented his loyalty to the firm.

Gideon was now caught between two great choices, each with different long-term implications for the likelihood and magnitude of financial success and non-financial rewards. There would never be a better opportunity to go out on his own: He had a proven idea, a winning track record, and the backing of two of the top private equity firms. Should he take the risk or let his entrepreneurial dream die?

It was too late to go back. The environment at Oppenheimer had been poisoned. Furthermore, Gideon did not wish to alienate Brownstein and Brody, who had steadily backed him through all the tumult. Gideon picked up the phone and made the definitive call: He was with them. By that point, they had completed all the new firm's documentation requirements, and Dave Stein could finally quit Harris and join Gideon. Two days later, "Gartner Group" was a reality!

Opco's End Run

The "group" part of the Gartner Group name was in fact a little misleading, since it was composed of only Gideon and Dave.

Since the bombshell meeting, Steve Robert had attempted to create a wedge between Gideon and Oppenheimer's Aaron Orlansky and Bill McAffery. It wasn't difficult to do; Orlansky was already smarting because Gideon had been leaning heavily on him about productivity. Opco had not counted on the success of Gideon's business-within-a-business — McAffery thought Oppenheimer was entirely *too* engrossed in the new business at the expense of its institutional clients. Orlansky had not taken this well.

Steve Robert planned to use these difficulties against Gideon. Oppenheimer promised Orlansky a brand new deal, based upon the contracts with the various firms who had already signed up for Gideon's Oppenheimer newsletter. After all, the contracts had been signed in Oppenheimer's name, not Gideon's; if Gideon went ahead and left Opco, he could kiss those clients goodbye. Steve Robert intended to fight for the business. He rightly surmised that any legal judgment would be in the incumbent's favor because the contracts were in Oppenheimer's name, a fact Gideon had admittedly overlooked. However, when it won the court case, Oppenheimer would need one or two people, at least, to fulfill these business obligations – and there, waiting in the wings, were Orlansky and McAffery.

Gideon and Dave quickly huddled to discuss whether to try to bring Orlansky and McAffery into Gartner Group. Their hope was that it might draw more clients to switch their allegiance to Gartner. They always held that maintaining continuity of service and allowing more clients the opportunity to be part of the new Gartner Group had to be the goal of any major changes. The Gartner brand was everything and would determine the fate of these two brilliant analysts.

But events had moved past the point of no return. Orlansky felt wounded at being left out of Gideon's early discussions with the VCs; he didn't understand why he hadn't been included in Gideon's initial plans. The reason, Gideon said, was simple: "Orlansky was brilliant but typical of many Wall Street analysts, he was an unguided missile. Nobody trusted him very much, including the Opco sales force. While security analysts are not known for their restraint in ferreting out inside – in fact, privileged – information about the companies they followed, there were limits. There had recently been some suggestion that Orlansky was at least at the limit, if not beyond, from an ethical perspective."

Gideon and Dave had a few discussions with Orlansky and McAffery to test their commitment to Oppenheimer. "I suspect that if Orlansky had accepted a junior partnership in our new company at that time, we might have gone along despite our better judgment – although Dave was even more skeptical than I was," Gideon recalled. But the battle lines were drawn. As Gideon and Dave thought through the variables again, they quickly agreed that they didn't want to consider a new option. "We both understood that we were losing a significant revenue opportunity, but we stuck to our guns with regard to the types we wished to hire," Gideon explained. He also hoped that he might be able to convince his old clients that they could, in fact, legally break their Opco contracts.

Off and Running

It was now April 1, 1979. Over the next month, Gideon and Dave called or visited most of their "hard dollar" clients, which included such big names as Xerox, Pepsico, and Procter & Gamble. Of the seventeen, only three were open to the idea of canceling their written contracts with Oppenheimer based upon staff changes and the loss of Gideon's research. Meanwhile, Opco was claiming that Gideon's replacements would soon provide the clients with similar research reports. Fourteen clients decided to sit tight, but ten of them told Gideon that after honoring their one-year contractual commitment to Opco, they would re-assess the situation when it came time to renew. "We had to accept the assumption that some but not all were quite pleased with what Orlansky and McAffery were delivering," Gideon said.

Three weeks later, the inexplicable occurred. Orlansky and McAffery quit Oppenheimer to join Dean Witter. "The two were obviously aware of their unpopularity with the Opco sales people, and must have questioned Opco's attitude towards them," Gideon explained. "Also, they obviously assumed that Dean Witter would inherit most of the Oppenheimer contracts. But they did not count on what immediately transpired."

Within hours of their quitting, Opco's research manager Bert Fingerhut phoned Gideon at home, asking him to travel downtown to his office ASAP. Gideon rushed to the Opco offices, where Bert disclosed that Orlansky and McAffery had just quit and probably expected to inherit the contracts. "We immediately negotiated and swiftly signed a straightforward deal whereby Opco would sign over all of its contracts to our new company, Gartner Group, in exchange for a 15 percent royalty to Opco which would decline to zero over a two-year period," Gideon recalled.

Back when Gideon first started his journey on Wall Street, a popular advertising tag line was, "When E.F. Hutton talks, people listen." Now, Gideon hoped, the shoe would be on the other foot. When Gartner Group spoke, E.F. Hutton *and* Oppenheimer *and* the entire IT industry would listen – and pay dearly for the information.

Gartner Group was off and running.

Senior Management Team, with Gideon in back row

Sales Team at a trade show

100

Chapter 8: The Gartner Group Brand

No one would ever describe Gideon as patient, least of all himself. "My inclination is to get everything up and running at once," he said. "So on Day One, we launched three newsletters, one each for investors, users and vendors."

Gartner Group's board of directors was aghast – "Gideon, you can't start three businesses at once!" – but, in fact, the three-pronged approach had been part of Gideon's plan from the very beginning: Produce high-quality analysis of news and trends in the rapidly growing tech industry, then customize and sell the research output not only to vendors of computer products and services, but simultaneously to users of such products and services, as well as to investors (mutual funds, insurance companies and institutional investment firms).

Gideon believed in the power of synergy. The standard operating procedure in those days was to sell such information only to vendors. Gideon knew that his firm's deep knowledge and intimate understanding of each constituency and its issues would continually be enriched through dealings with all three, creating precisely the multifaceted conclusions that were often promised but had never yet been delivered to customers in the market information industry.

There is little doubt that this set Gartner Group apart from the other research firms and helped it leapfrog the competition. But there were other differentiators, too.

From the beginning, Gartner's hiring policy was unique. When Gartner's competition went looking for a new analyst, the companies tended to hire bright but relatively junior MBAs with slight technical backgrounds. Gartner was looking for tech experts. "Companies like IDC or Dataquest hired smart but junior people because they were essentially sizing markets," Gideon explained. "Their role was to look only at the market aspects of the companies they covered" – not the technology aspects and certainly not the user aspects, which was very important in Gartner's strategy. So, Gideon set out to hire the most experienced analysts he could possibly find. He particularly liked taking people out of the vendor community, especially those who understood their competition and the dynamics of their sector. To be sure, these people tended to be expensive, but they were worth the price. "Our people were great," Gideon said. "The marketplace had not seen people like that."

Another facet of the brand Gartner was building was the firm's solid commitment to a thorough research process—the firm not only presented data, but analyzed it. While competitors focused mainly on numbers, Gartner Group focused on what the numbers meant. While others examined the nuts and bolts of technology developments, Gartner zeroed in on the probable impact of these developments on business issues and on a company's bottom line. Competitors tended to use hit-or-miss research methods, whereas Gideon designed and standardized his group's process. This documented method strengthened the firm's research culture, creating uniformity in its deliverables, enhancing its brand, and impressing its clients.

Gideon's insistence on a strict discipline using established standards rigorously applied when making financial projections to the industry lent a much needed dose of reality to market research, and differentiated Gartner Group's projections from what sometimes sounded like wishful thinking from their competitors. Gideon recalled, "We scored a hit in developing a mathematical model which correlated the future residual values of mainframe computers to how long it would take for the machines to become obsolete, thus aiding user clients in their rent vs. purchase decisions. Some employees claimed that this single innovation was critical in jump-starting our business. It certainly was an important factor."

The firm's unique research process sounded theoretical but worked brilliantly. Gideon soon drafted a Research Manual, which, through several iterations over the years, became the basis of a series of courses, which were taught to all incoming analysts. The process centered on a seemingly-simple dictum:

Scan as many sources as possible in order to recognize patterns among companies, markets, and industries.

The companies whose analysts were expected to scan included IBM and DEC, but went down to the new start-ups. Gideon expected his analysts to stay on top of the news, to know what was opening and closing and what that meant. "Markets" included software, or the value-added distribution channel. And when Gideon spoke of "industries" he meant hard drives, or enterprise management software, for example. His analysts needed to read broadly and profusely, to have a large network of differentiated sources, and to unabashedly remain curious about each and every aspect of the marketplace—and most importantly, to have the innate intelligence to bring disparate threads of data together and weave them into a meaningful narrative that a busy investor could grasp in an instant.

Through this process of surmising, deducing, and concluding from large bodies of seemingly unrelated and inconclusive information, analysts were expected to demonstrate both left-brain thinking (logical analysis) and right-brain thinking (flashes of insight).

Once a conclusion was reached, it was drawn up and presented in research meetings through what became known as a *stalking horse*. The stalking horse was so integral to the Gartner research process that the horse became the firm's conceptual mascot. Gideon eventually amassed an extensive collection of horse art for the building: paintings, sculptures, even a large, colorful pastel drawn by his young daughter Sabrina.

And what was a stalking horse? A stalking horse referred to an amorphous idea just waiting to crystallize into an indelible conclusion. Gideon's stalking horse invention was a simple 2x2 graphic diagram, which he called "the magic quadrant," which compared one vendor's or product's strengths and weaknesses to those of its competition.[6]

"Everyone wanted to be in the upper right quadrant," recalled Peter Wright, an early hire who became one of the firm's star analysts. The magic quadrants, or MQs, as they were known, were presented at the Gartner research meetings where the analyst's pitch was subjected to ferocious debate that picked apart all the weaknesses and refined the strengths of the analyst's conclusions. These conclusions then coalesced into the seemingly simple two-sided document called the *green sheet*.

The Green Sheets

Gartner's competition tended to write long-winded, comprehensive reports. These were delivered at random times, and more often than not, would languish on clients' credenzas, collecting dust, or holding up volumes of similar treatises. Gideon designed his green sheets to be both readable and succinct. "He always wanted to

---

[6] "3 Things You Need to Know About Gartner Magic Quadrants," by Richard Stiennon. *CIO*, July 6, 2012.

make sure that the reader would take away a message," said Peter Wright. Knowing the limited attention span of his audience, Gideon emphasized brevity. His repeated injunction: "If I can't finish the page while I'm taking a piss, then it's way too long."

The format was always the same: one page, two sides only. The opening paragraph could be no more than two sentences. The basic content, its summary and advice all had to fit on one side of the page. The other side was reserved for graphs and tables, always presenting the information in as straightforward a manner as possible. Because these notes were photocopied onto green paper, they were known as *green sheets*. They became a Gartner Group trademark.

Dick Imershein, Gideon's former IBM colleague who joined Gartner Group in 1980, surmised that Gideon's insistence on concise writing stemmed from writing opera reviews for *The Brooklyn Eagle* when he was a senior at Midwood High School. Gideon was a buddy of Bob Lesserson, another high school entrepreneur who published a free paper and played second French horn chair in Midwood's orchestra, next to Gideon's first chair. Together they decided that most people didn't want an in-depth discussion of opera and didn't care whether the conductor sneezed or fell off the podium. They just wanted to know the net: who sang well, who sang badly, how the performers performed, and whether the overall music was good. Similarly at Gartner, Gideon realized his clients were not interested in "diarrhea-of-the-mouth" in the marketplace. They wanted information that didn't need to be translated, that didn't use "geek" words, that was understandable – and that's what Gartner's reports gave them.

Some of the analysts who were hired during Gartner's early days complained bitterly that an arbitrary limit of one page was constraining and would hurt quality. Gideon refused to buckle, although he eventually compromised – ever so slightly – by telling them that if necessary, they could "split" their written analysis into stand-alone chunks labeled Part 1 and Part 2 – and even Part 3. But Gideon recalled, "I don't think that caught on much." Gideon's "keep it simple, stupid" directive ensured that the analyst's message got through.

Revenue and compensation

While the competition measured its financial progress via its revenues, Gartner Group focused on the "annualized dollar value" of the installed client base at any given point in time and, even more importantly, on the growth of this dollar value during specific periods of time, e.g., monthly, quarterly, and yearly. Sales commissions and companywide bonuses were based primarily on growth increments as measured by net new business on top of the starting base, and *not* on revenues for the period – in other words, people were oriented to focus not on revenues but on the *growth* of revenues. This was not an entirely new concept, but applying it as Gideon did was a major factor in Gartner Group's enormous success.

Gartner was a subscription business. "We would charge an annual retainer for a bundle of content plus events plus telephonic support, all of which the client would receive via various forms of packaging," Gideon explained. "We would create sales territories where a salesperson's compensation for a period of time was dependent only upon the growth of his or her territory, instead of on the revenue which the territory produced. And, other people in the company – both in the U.S. and abroad – would also be measured on net increases in the business segment they were responsible for."

In most recurring revenue business models, the sales force is divided into what some call *hunters and farmers:* Hunters get paid for the new clients and farmers renew existing clients. "Gideon took a different tack," Peter Wright noted. "He wanted his sales people to see an unlimited opportunity to make money, but in order to do that, they had to renew what they already had." And woe betide any salesperson whose client base shrank. "If his or her base lost half a million, then the next year they would have to renew their contact base *and* get new clients," Peter said. "They had to row a leaky boat *and* bail." The trick, Peter explained, was always to increase the salesman's bag by introducing new products, but at the same time Gideon and his sales managers were hiring new salesmen and narrowing the salespeople's territories.

The overall result was to make the sales force responsible for the product they were selling. "This approach ultimately led us to triple or quadruple our sales productivity, and enabled us to invest in what would become the sharpest sales organization in our industry," Gideon said.

In addition, unlike other firms, which were controlled by a single entrepreneur with much closely held stock, Gartner Group distributed stock broadly within the company. This generosity greatly improved morale and helped create a financial structure that enabled employees to invest in the firm and grow with it, even at the expense of early year profits. These strategies strengthened Gartner and its unique growth culture, and were key factors in Gartner Group's continuing growth and market share expansion, even during soft economies.

Strong Backing

Venture capitalists Neill Brownstein and Chris Brody did more than merely fund Gartner Group. They provided deep financial insight and moral support through the various ups and downs of the young company's development. Their support helped the fledgling firm gain financial strength, industry connections, and the credibility critical to its long-term success.

Gideon soon felt an additional cash buffer was needed – "I perceived a huge mountain of debt looming above us," he recalled – so Chris and Neill made the introduction to Paribas, the large French commercial bank. "Paribas was frank in telling us that its investment departments were interested in receiving all our research, which reminded me that this had been one of the major incentives for Bessemer and Warburg to invest in us in the first place," Gideon noted. The bank made a $500,000 equity investment.

The VCs' credibility enabled Gartner Group to attract an effective board of directors. The original board of Gideon and Dave Stein, Neill and Chris, was soon joined by two heavyweights: Harry Steinberg, executive vice president of Univac, and Professor Jim Emery of Wharton School of Business.

"Neill and Chris complemented each other beautifully," Gideon said. "They were both whole-brained people but Neill was stronger on the right side of the brain and an expansive thinker, while Chris was a strong left-brainer and a detailed nitpicker. Overall, a great combination. They were on target in a remarkably high percentage of their inputs, while of course representing their own interests to the nth degree. They were also nice guys, even though as financial heavies, niceness didn't always mix with business judgments. Most important, they were both indefatigable and willing to go out of their way to help the business. Neill became a close friend over the years and was always willing to extend himself on a personal level as well as on a business level."

Early Days

Chris Brody also helped engineer Gartner Group's first coup. Realizing that the firm needed a distribution channel for its Wall Street research, he initiated conversations with the Dillon Read

Corporation, then one of the top boutique firms on Wall Street. Within three months, Chris convinced it to become the content distribution agent for Gartner Group's Wall Street practice, which was called Gartner Securities. Gideon noted, "Of course, we had an edge compared with other Wall Street analysts in the tech space, because a significant percentage of the research Gartner Group would be producing for our vendors and users could be re-focused towards the interests of Wall Street. This was consistent with our original rationale for creating a firm which would immediately market to the three constituencies (vendor, user, investor), each of which would benefit from our understanding of the other two, where we would understand all three and where we would also benefit from considerable content overlap."

Dillon Read agreed to pay $500,000 per annum to serve as the distribution agent. The relationship lasted five years, with the figure growing by $500,000 each year until it hit $3 million, "after which we built our own trading desk and sales force for institutional investors, and called the business Soundview Financial," Gideon recalled.

Dillon Read also purchased six percent of Gartner Group's business and provided office space in its headquarters on 46 William Street– there was just enough room for Gideon and Dave Stein, with a secretary in the hallway.

Karen Healy was one of the first ten hires. "I had responded to Gideon's advertisement in a local Westchester County paper for an administrative assistant to the CEO of a start-up company that would soon be moving to Greenwich, Connecticut," she recalled. "We arranged to meet at Sassafras, a restaurant in Mamaroneck. I was driving my Triumph 206 up Mamaroneck Avenue, and at the stoplight I looked to my left and saw some guy in a Triumph convertible who glanced at me. When I got to the restaurant, I discovered it was Gideon.

"We talked about his business and it was very foreign to me. I had been working for a German import/export company, so it was a stretch for me to understand when he talked about IBM mainframes and the residual values of computers. But, as coincidence would have it, I had been doing a search for office space in and around Greenwich for my existing employer and had a lot of information on the real estate market in that area."

Karen started working for Gartner Group in September 1979; she became a lifelong friend to Gideon. She found the set-up at 46 William Street "kind of amusing." Gideon and Dave shared one office, stuffed with file cabinets. Four analysts were in the other room, their desks crammed cheek by jowl. Karen and another secretary were in the hallway, typing up the analysts' research notes on a plain piece of white paper. Then they would take them to the Dillon Read mailroom and have them photocopied onto green paper – the green sheets.

By November 1979, the firm – now with nine employees – moved to Greenwich, which Gideon thought would be more attractive for recruiting purposes, especially when new employees would be moving with their families from out of town. The office was on Steamboat Road, right next to Manero's Restaurant, a steak-and-pasta joint which added its own special flavor to the environment. "We smelled fried onions and cheeseburgers all day," Karen recalled. The firm was growing so fast that before long, everyone was doubling up in offices again; less than two years later, Gartner Group again moved to larger quarters.

More Culture Shock

Despite the presence of many former IBMers, no one would ever confuse Gartner Group with buttoned-down Big Blue. For starters, there was no dress code.

Scott Smith recounted the story of his interview for the position of Gideon's executive assistant. In the middle of the interview, a scruffy young guy with an unruly beard, dressed in ripped jeans and a worn flannel shirt, wandered into the office. "I stopped talking mid-sentence," Smith recalled. "Gideon immediately wondered what was wrong. I replied that I was waiting for the maintenance man to leave. Gideon laughed and explained that the 'maintenance man' was Peter Wright, then the #3 manager at Gartner and a top producer. My view of the business world was forever changed." This story became a treasured piece of Gartner Group lore.

At a time long before Silicon Valley normalized sloppiness at work, a sign in the lobby would warn when clients would be coming in to meet with analysts, so that people would know to dress appropriately. Otherwise, casual dress – in some cases, *very* casual – was the rule.

The cutthroat politics of an established corporation were nonexistent in the frantic start-up atmosphere. "Everyone was going a hundred miles per hour in all different directions. You'd get rewarded for hard work and your contributions," Peter said. "You were allowed to move in any direction you wanted, so if you were creative and entrepreneurial, you had a chance as a young professional to be successful and not have politics be an impediment to making an impact."

The working arrangements were an analyst's dream. While analysts were free to talk to institutional clients and clients were welcome to call them, they weren't mired in the presentations to salespeople and clients that had taken up more than eighty percent of Gideon's time at Oppenheimer. Aided by a phalanx of muscular IBM mainframes and working at custom-designed desks, once the office eventually moved to Stamford, Connecticut, analysts could indulge in the kind of research they never had time for in the past.

That's not to say that the analysts lolled about in research paradise. It was a work hard/play hard atmosphere. The hours could be brutal: Long days were for producing and after-hours, including weekends, for staff meetings. Because analysts were measured on productivity – how many research notes they wrote and how many inquiries they answered from clients – 70-hour weeks were normal.

People often arrived for work at 7:30 a.m. and worked until 8 or 9 at night, then went for a drink, and returned to the office. At first, Gideon was still living in New York, so rather than waste time commuting, he would simply crash on a cot in his office and spend the night. (Fortunately, his office had a shower.) Plenty of people followed his example. "People who didn't have energy didn't survive," Peter said. "You had to be able to produce efficiently and effectively."

The staff also had to have a thick skin. Research meetings were contentious, confrontational free-for-alls, with analysts arguing their points and disagreeing often at the top of their lungs. Gideon pointed out, "There was as much constructive criticism as destructive criticism." People called each other names and stormed out of the room. When Greg Somerville, the editor of the newsletter *Stock Market Innovators*, joined Gideon and a number of associates for the weekly luncheon meeting reviewing Gartner Securities' current investment positions, he was aghast. "It resembled a combination of group therapy and an encounter session," he wrote, "with no holds barred in open, frank and sometimes heated discussions of different companies and products. No 'yes men' here."[7]

Gideon himself fueled some of the mayhem. "He liked to be a wise guy," Peter Wright recalled. "Everyone would be going along in one direction in a research meeting and then he'd say, 'Has anyone

---

[7] *Stock Market Innovators*, October 1981.

considered this?' and bring up an important point that would totally change the direction of the discussion."

However, there was method in what often seemed like a madhouse. In the same *Stock Market Innovators* article, Somerville noted, "After spending several hours with Mr. Gartner discussing his firm and the technology stock group, it became quite clear that this laid-back atmosphere and unregimented environment disguise[d] one of the most intensive and sophisticated investment research operations in the world." The same aversion to groupthink was also imbued in Gartner Group's technology research process. Despite all the drama, Peter recalled, the atmosphere never turned bitter. It was, at heart, collegial and collaborative. "People were emotional but no one held grudges," he said.

In his search for independent-minded and creative new hires, Gideon would put job candidates through a gauntlet. "When we interviewed somebody for a job, there was a group interview, never one-on-one interviews. We threw snowballs at the interviewee." For example, fully knowing that IBM was still the major factor in the industry, Gideon recalled asking one interviewee, "'Stand up at the white board and make a presentation as to how you think IBM might lose money within two years and then go bankrupt within five.' It was a completely stupid question but it forced the guy to think outside the box and construct some kind of a scenario. It could be because of a legal action, a combination of God-knows-what, some one-chance-in-a-thousand scenario, but it had to be reasonably plausible. The interviewee would have to be able to think on his or her feet and present effectively."

Looking back, Gideon could be compared to another tech industry iconoclast working at the same time on the West Coast. Like Steve Jobs, Gideon followed the beat of his own drummer. "Gideon always had innovative ways of doing things," Karen Healy said. "He was always thinking outside the box." Unlike Dave Stein, whom many described as Gideon's alter-ego – a traditional, process-driven, by-the-book guy – Gideon was, as Peter Wright put it, "very helter-skelter but extraordinarily creative."

One of Gideon's most revolutionary and controversial innovations was to ban all slide presentations. PowerPoint had yet to be invented, and he thought that too many people used slides as a crutch, cramming them with too much information in barely legible type, and then just stood in front of an audience and read from them, Karen recalled. So one day, Gideon announced, "Forget it, we're not doing slides."

He had made the pronouncement just before a conference. "Everyone complained about it," Karen remembered, "but it was effective, because it got people interacting with the audience. There are even people today who use that technique because it's more effective."

Gideon himself was a showman nonpareil. Rather than using static slides for presentations, he made his points memorable by simultaneously talking and sketching on an overhead projector —

trend charts, graphs, and his trademark "magic quadrant" —
comparing industry innovators to laggards in terms of price and
performance.

One time, Gideon was at the Ritz Hotel in Paris, about to make a
presentation to a group of French clients, when to his dismay, he
discovered that the overhead projector hadn't been delivered. Like
many of the formal meeting rooms in Paris' *grand hôtels particuliers,*
the walls were lined with mirrors. "I thought quickly and asked the
few ladies in attendance whether I could borrow a lipstick," Gideon
recalled. One volunteered. "I took the lipstick, moved to the
beautiful gilded mirror in the room and proceeded to draw my
trend graphs and market forecasts on the surface. When the hotel
service people saw what I had done, they were apoplectic!" But the
clients applauded – and the episode became Gartner Group lore.

Karen Healy reminisced, "What made it fun was working hard and
seeing the results of your efforts." As the company rapidly
expanded, she moved into increasingly bigger roles with greater
responsibility. "I was able to build much of the infrastructure
because we started with nothing. I developed a word-processing
department, because we needed people to type the analysts' reports.
I built the entire production department that went from
photocopying reports to having a big facility managed by Xerox,
printing out millions of copies."

Gartner Group innovated with its internal culture as well. The
cafeteria offerings were converted from the usual fare to health

food. Instead of telephone Muzak, callers who were put on hold listened to Chopin – sometimes played by Gideon.

The idea was work hard, play hard.

"It was an intense place to work," said Peter Wright. "But the reward was your ability to create."

Delivering the Goods

Many young firms can't handle success; they try to do too much, too soon, and lose control. What kept Gartner Group on course through its explosive early growth was that its compass setting never varied. Even as its green sheets begat in-depth monthly analyses on major topics, and client presentations led to half-day, then full-day conferences, then multi-day extravaganzas, and the info-tech industry itself began to sparkle and pop like Fourth of July fireworks, demanding that Gartner Group pile on more and more brainpower to keep up, the firm stayed true to its fundamental mission: using documentation and discussion to analyze trends in the information industry and advise its three groups of clients accordingly.

At first, Gartner's deliverable was called the Residual Asset Value Information System (RAVIS) and the advice, based on Dave Stein's mathematical model, helped customers assess whether they should rent or buy their computers from IBM, then the sole provider of large-scale mainframe computers. This sort of asset management advice was an easy sell to many users because it demonstrated how they could save money. "The clients basically paid by the drink," Gideon explained. Gartner Group's next original package was a group of deliverables priced at $20,000 annually: It included the green sheets, several significantly larger reports, tickets to a Gartner Group conference, and unlimited calls to a Gartner Group analyst.

As technology changed and networking became important, Gideon introduced a second $20,000 service, offering similar elements as the RAVIS but with orange sheets instead of green, addressing networking issues and billed separately. This too, was very profitable, and it soon became a trend in the company, as each major innovation in the industry spawned another Gartner Group service to evaluate the products, predict its trends, and counsel its vendors, users and investors.

"There were 200 vendors but 2,000 users and they had insatiable appetites," recalled Peter Wright. But the basic strategy stayed the same: as Gideon explained, "to put together a package of services that the clients will find irresistible."

And they did.

Revenues the first year topped $600,000, then more than doubled to $1.6 million the next. Within three years of its founding, Gartner Group had sixty people on staff – half of them analysts – and boasted sixty-five large enterprise clients, paying annual fees of up to $70,000 each. Annual revenues again doubled to $3.2

million. At the end of four years, Gartner Group was pulling in
$5.8 million.

Reinventing the Industry

"I'm here to tell you, Gartner Group is like nothing the computer
industry has seen before," wrote Portia Isaacson Wright in a 1988
issue of *Future Thinker* entirely devoted to Gartner Group – the
newsletter reviewed published market research and business
information in the computer, telecommunications, semiconductor,
and office products industries.[8] "It's too easy to characterize
Gartner Group as something we already know. It's not. At the very
least, Gartner Group has reinvented market information
publishing. We will all benefit, some more painfully than others."

In addition, she warned, "Market research companies who have
made a living lining the shelves of libraries in high-tech vendor
and user companies, take heed – times are a'changin'! Once buyers
get used to it, they'll think all market research should be this way."

Peter Wright compared the impact of Gartner Group to the
introduction of Lotus 123, the spreadsheet program that was the first
"killer app" for PCs. Although the market for personal computers
wasn't very big, PCs already existed; the problem was that most
people didn't know what to do with them. "Then an application like
a spreadsheet comes along, and now people know what to do with
it," Wright said. But, he pointed out, there was a significant

---

[8] *Future Thinker*, September 1, 1998.

difference: "Selling strategic information? It took someone's imagination to create a market that didn't really exist. The market wasn't driven by a product. Rather, it was driven by convincing people that there were opportunities to make better decisions – or to have consultants help you make even better decisions – that were productive and financially measurable. Because of Gartner Group," he concluded, "the world morphed from operational and product research to strategic consulting research."

"Gideon always had a plan," Karen Healy recalls. "He would draw charts and say, 'Here's our revenue now and here's what it's going to be in five years.' People would be saying, 'Are you kidding? We're never going to get there.' But we did."

Dick Imershein and Mark Ludwig

Chapter 9: Challenging IBM

The differences between Gartner Group and conventional research firms weren't limited to culture, compensation, and clothing. Thanks to its proprietary research process, Gartner produced advice that frequently contradicted conventional wisdom, often with dramatic results.

One of its most controversial calls came in the summer of 1981. The subject was Amdahl, then flying high as the top manufacturer of large plug-compatible mainframes. Amdahl's stock had soared to $31.75 per share by August 1981 and the Wall Street consensus was that in 1982, the company would earn one dollar per share. Gartner Group instead published its prediction that in 1982, Amdahl would barely earn $.20 per share and furthermore warned that it "might not make any money at all."

Gideon explained the reasons for such pessimism: "Amdahl's results hinged on its ability to deliver fifty of its new 5860 models in 1982. If shipments were delayed until 1983, earnings would suffer. Our analysts had checked and discovered that *none* of the shipments had confirmed delivery dates. Furthermore, they found that a key supplier had a schedule conflict and might delay shipment of an essential sub-assembly. In addition, we expected IBM to introduce a product that would hurt another of Amdahl's product lines." Bucking the trend, Gartner issued the first Wall Street "sell" recommendation on Amdahl's stock in August 1981;

by the following June, the stock was trading at $17.75. Gideon later noted that Amdahl had an outstanding year in 1983 – "and we called that one, too!" he laughed.

Gartner's Growing Influence

Accurate calls like these helped raise and burnish the young firm's reputation. Gartner Group began to affect the development and sales of information technology significantly. But, despite its knowledge of users' requirements, Gartner's impact on vendors' product plans was relatively marginal. So Gideon declared, "Our new goals were to enable vendors to understand their competition better, so we could be like a competitive analysis department for the vendors."

For users, Gartner Group's advice was becoming invaluable. "We focused on saving them money by helping them make better acquisitions decisions," Gideon explained. "We provided decision support when they had issues about internal configurations, about which platforms to use, and about interconnectivity of the whole growing kludge of software. But equally important, we focused also on their relationship with vendors. Over time, users began to rely more and more on these assessments in their evaluation of vendors, especially small vendors who were coming on stream in new niches within the market." Gartner Group trained a close focus on the obsolescence rates of equipment that was on the market: noting how long equipment lasted before it was replaced and the functionality and price performance metrics of the next generation of equipment that would replace it. "The fact that we took positions on the time frame of when a piece of hardware would be replaced by the next generation and what the specs would be helped determine the level of obsolescence of the existing equipment, especially if that equipment was yet not installed but was in the pipeline waiting to be acquired by the customer. So we influenced buying decisions to a great extent."

Throughout the 1970s and into the early 80s, the largest vendor of technology was IBM. Big Blue ruled the info-tech industry and vendors and users alike danced around IBM like courtiers at Louis XIV's Versailles. When IBM made a product announcement, *everyone* listened.

Given IBM's industry dominance, Gartner Group naturally devoted many resources to deciphering Big Blue's strategies. Gideon explained, "If we felt that a replacement series was scheduled within a six-month time frame of an existing product, it wouldn't make much sense for an IBM client to purchase the current models, especially if the forthcoming product had a substantially improved price-to-performance ratio, which it likely often would." The result: A client would postpone the acquisition or would rent instead of buying (in fact, IBM's rental business overshadowed its outright sales).

IBM was already under attack from designers and manufacturers of IBM-compatible mainframes (such as Amdahl and the Japanese) that were trying to penetrate its huge installed base of large systems, which was its major revenue source. As more of IBM's customers followed Gartner advice, rather than dancing to IBM's tune, Gartner Group morphed from an annoying gadfly to becoming a significant threat to Big Blue's business.

IBM Responds

In the spring of 1982, Gartner Group predicted that IBM would lower mainframe purchase prices in the fall. This information was promptly disseminated to all of its user clients who were contemplating mainframe purchases. This strategic advice brought sales of IBM mainframes to a screeching halt that summer.

With many ex-IBMers now working at Gartner – the roster included co-founder Dave Stein, Dick Imershein (Senior Vice President), Dorothy Langer (VP of Sales and Marketing) and, of course, Gideon, just to name a few of the senior people – the possibilities for being party to inside information were rife. But IBM had no evidence to back up any serious claims to sue the firm for *that* reason.

A year later, however, it found another.

In early March, 1983, Gideon received a visit from Tom Barr, the top lawyer at IBM's law firm, Cravath Swaine & Moore, and Nicholas Katzenbach, former U.S. Attorney General and now General Counsel for IBM. "I was calmly and respectfully told that copies of Gartner presentation charts were found stapled to IBM 'Confidential—Do Not Copy' documents during discovery

126

proceedings in an ongoing lawsuit between IBM and National Semiconductor," Gideon recalled. "These white-shoe lawyers announced that IBM believed that we had obtained IBM confidential documents, and were distributing them to our clients – stapled to our Green Sheets! Naturally, my esteemed visitors said we were not the subject of an investigation or the target of litigation, and were skeptical that we were the source of this material. Nevertheless, they asked me respectfully to look into this. Imagine how shocked and nervous I felt!"

People at Gartner Group knew that "IBM Confidential" was then IBM's lowest form of security rating (below "IBM Secret," "IBM Top Secret," etc.) and that the source of the IBM Confidential document was an IBM classroom where dozens of documents were exchanged with little further security control. However, IBM now had Gartner Group in its sights; Gideon recalled, "Despite Big Blue's initial representations, we were on the brink of being sued over distributing 'illegally obtained confidential IBM documents to Gartner clients'—very serious stuff!"

The matter was settled out of court. But as part of the consent, all Gartner Group employees received and had to sign a document describing IBM's demands for their future behavior. Representatives from Weil Gotshal, Gartner Group's law firm, assured IBM they would visit Gartner annually to review the obligations of the settlement with all analysts. Finally, Gartner Group had to agree to what was called in the trade a "snitch clause," whereby any offer by an outsider to provide any information which might possibly be considered confidential would have to be reported immediately to IBM counsel.

Ironically, the aftermath of IBM's suit resulted in Gartner Group becoming an even greater force in the industry. Wall Street analysts began to question the usual tendency to revere and admire Big Blue and, Gideon recalled, "began to call a spade a spade whenever possible," although Gideon emphasized that he required hard evidence whenever a Gartner report seemed to "bash" IBM.

Reshaping the Computer Industry

Throughout the 1980s, turbulence roiled the computer industry. The traditional vertical mode, epitomized by IBM, in which a single company designed, produced and put together all the components of a product, was shifting to a horizontal model in which different companies manufactured specific components at sharply reduced prices. New competitors were emerging and grabbing market share at a frightening rate. In a shockingly short period of time, IBM, the world's most successful, most profitable, most powerful, most influential, and best-managed company, was reduced to just another huge corporation struggling to adjust to forces beyond its control.

Gartner Group played a significant role in this fundamental reshaping of the computer industry, not through any sense of vengeance against IBM but simply because of the strength of its research model and how its advice affected strategic decisions by users, vendors and institutional investors. Here's how the firm made an impact:

- AS AN OBSERVER: No other firm chronicled IBM's deterioration more comprehensively than Gartner Group (despite Gideon's insistence that analysts be objective. "Our growing client base of Fortune 500 firms were certainly aware of the issues," Gideon noted. "Ironically, they became important sources of information! For example, our intimate knowledge of the mainframe leasing space – where we were doing business with all the major players – also provided strong insights which often saved our clients hundreds of thousands of dollars or more by helping them fine-tune their transactions with IBM."

- AS AN ANALYST: With IBM as Gartner Group's largest client still, and with many of the firm's employees ex-IBMers with strong residual loyalties, the firm was in a position to explicitly help adjudicate IBM's strategic alternatives both via the client relationship which IBM was paying for and also through focused consulting relationships. Gideon's reputation from his Wall Street days as "the" IBM watcher also helped establish Gartner Group's credibility. "Yet while knowing of our expertise and tight connections to virtually all its largest clients, IBM never once asked for our help or even our opinions," Gideon noted. "IBM was oblivious to our comments to clients – including, of course, our financial clients – that we saw its decision to sell off its rental base in order to manage its earnings as a likely future Waterloo."

• As a catalyst: "Our responsibility was to our clients, not just to IBM," Gideon stipulated. He explained, "While IBM was a major client, it was just one of many and we needed to analyze the industry objectively." Throughout this period, Gartner Group educated the marketplace, giving users who had formerly felt obliged to respond to IBM's every whim the confidence to assert their independence from Big Blue. Gartner also served as the first-ever "inside information switch," as the firm's multiple relationships with large user organizations such as the Society for Information Management (or SIM, whose members included chief information officers and other IT executives from around the world) helped inform its customer base of the special deals which others were now obtaining from other manufacturers. That, in turn, made such deals almost universally available considerably faster than would have happened by natural evolution (especially since IBM in the 1970s had been a fixed-price, no-deal vendor). Gartner Group's research gave IBM's customers confidence and reassurance when they considered switching to other vendors, such as mid- to large-range manufacturers like Digital Equipment Corporation, Burroughs, Control Data, Cray Research, Four Phase Systems, SDS (Scientific Data Systems) and plug-compatible manufacturers like Amdahl, Hitachi, Fujitso, Memorex, Telex and others who copied IBM's technologies and invariably sold them at a lower price.

The Decline of IBM

"Via a combination of company contacts, but mostly through analysis, we forecast aspects of IBM's impending product announcements, which of course tended to freeze the market for its soon-to-be-obsolete platforms," Gideon recalled. This added to IBM's financial woes to the point that after one particularly prescient report from Gartner Group, IBM's chief financial officer called Gideon in Paris to complain, "Gideon, do you realize what you've done to the company's quarterly earnings?"

"IBM's paranoia led them to suspect that we were again obtaining privileged information," Gideon said. "Perhaps there was a 'very marginal' hint of truth to the rumor, but the reality was the power of Gartner Group's research process and our ability to triangulate inputs, which of course led to reasonable predictions of when and to what extent IBM would need to upgrade its various models." Still, Big Blue remained concerned, although its vigilance was occasionally tempered by a sense of humor: It was said in Armonk, IBM's corporate headquarters, that a standing joke was, "Have you spoken to Gideon lately?"

Even as outside events and developments contributed to IBM's decline throughout the 1980s, Big Blue itself blundered as a consequence of its own overly complex marketing ploys, its overselling, and its development delays. At the same time, such errors prompted and enabled waves of attacks from competitors, resulting in measurable shifts in user attitudes. Gideon commented, "IBM had access but had it also listened carefully to us, it might have done a better job of maintaining aspects of its industry leadership. Our involvement could clearly be shown through what we published and verbally communicated to our customers, based upon direct research interactions with IBM and also by listening to our mutual customers. I believe that Gartner will be remembered as the principle influencer of its customers' decisions and trust that most, if not all, of our information was effectively public. Of course, there was lots of loose talk in this competitive industry!"

This was certainly a profound shift in the information technology industry: that a relatively small consulting firm, with connections to many important client decision makers, had an explicit, broad, and sometimes overriding decision-support effect.

When its earnings were pressured in the late '80s, IBM began to sell off the large systems, which had been part of its vast rental pool. IBM's policy of renting, rather than selling, its equipment had been critical to creating and maintaining financial stability. Gideon's take? "Ironically, at Gartner Group I copied – in a somewhat modified form – IBM's sales compensation and incentive program, which was based upon the advantages of a recurring revenue model enabled by its dominant position in the vast rental pool. IBM's 'NSRI' (Net Sales Record Increase), based upon the incremental annual performance increase in each salesperson's territory, was the measurement that drove the IBM sales force to meet their quotas. We frankly copied it with our 'NCVI' (Net Contract Value Increase) system. In both cases, no compensation was offered for the value of the installed base of a territory, only of its growth. Our sales executives were mainly compensated on the increase (or decrease) in the dollar value of installations in his or her territory. Thus, in both cases, the entire company's progress was tied to increases in customer contracts. We were beholden to IBM in this regard!"

Selling off this rich rental pool eventually led to volatility and earnings instability. To the IBM-watchers at Gartner Group, nothing could have been more obvious. As IBM's decisions to manage short-term versus long-term earning power led to its decline, Gartner Group chronicled every step of its demise through green sheets and other reports. In fact, one of the top analysts, Peter Wright, boldly predicted that IBM would eventually experience negative quarterly results. "In those days, that was heresy!" Gideon recalled. "We scoffed at that internally – but Peter was proved right! Of course, we would never switch from a rental to a sales system."

134

Chapter 10: Think Tank

"Are you a guru?"

Richard Ross was working at a tech start-up when he spotted an advertisement in *The Boston Globe* asking that enigmatic question. Finding the answer led him from Boston's humming tech corridor to the lush suburbs of Stamford, headquarters of Gartner Group. Ross recalled, "In quick succession, I was introduced to some of the smartest people I had ever met. Gideon Gartner was all pizzazz with a sharp edge. Dave Stein could start talking about how a chip is made and take you through the evolution of the computer industry and the resulting ramifications for the global economy for the next 100 years. Dick Imershein had worked at IBM so long that his career was the computer industry."

Ultimately, what won Ross over was his interview with Steve Cohen. Cohen, like many of Gartner's top lieutenants, was an ex-IBMer who was running the firm's flagship Industry Service (IS) section. Wearing a very un-corporate outfit of jeans and sports shirt, Steve ushered the dazzled young prospect into his office, leaned back in his chair and propped his Nike-clad feet on the desk. "We do two things here," he announced. "Make money and have a good time."

Richard Ross moved to Connecticut the following week to become the 13th member of Gartner's Information Services department. "I had no idea what I might be getting into," he recalled, "but I knew there was more to business than building stuff, and I wanted to see what was out there." Gartner Group was the perfect launch pad from which to explore this new world.

In August 1981, Gartner Group had moved from Greenwich to 72 Cummings Point Road in Stamford, Connecticut, overlooking the Long Island Sound and surrounded by rolling lawns dotted with rhododendrons and dogwood trees. By 1985, it was ranked the 163rd fastest growing private company in the United States, according to *Inc.* magazine. Its revenues exploded from $500,000 in 1979 to $20 million in 1985. The number of employees had also soared – from 20 in 1980 to 160 (and growing) in 1985 – and so had the client list: over 500 clients worldwide, with 160 of them *Fortune 500* firms. Gartner was pumping out over 10,000 pages a year of analysis. Its trademark two-sided green sheets now appeared in a veritable Crayola palette of colors, each of which designated areas ranging from minicomputers to PCs, from office information to telecommunications, as well as what Gartner called an "Industry Service" sector which extracted the essence of the other services, while adding an effective overview for the industry at large.

Gideon liked to refer to his firm as a think tank. In an interview with *MIT Management*, he said, "When people are about to make a decision, they call us to strengthen the courage of their convictions.

I think that is because we are a think tank, so to speak – although we're not an academic group – a concentration of very talented, very highly paid people on whom we have superimposed a way of doing things – a process, a style – which is somewhat refreshing and may challenge our clients' thought processes. The synergy that develops between our clients and ourselves often produces flashes of insight."

Gartner Group's free-wheeling, democratic management style that allowed flexible hours, informal dress codes, and a philosophy that treated its employees as equals and encouraged anyone to talk to everyone about anything attracted a distinct type of person – Gartner Groupies, as they were nicknamed – and fostered intense pride and a special camaraderie.

"The best part of working at Gartner Group was its people," Ross mused. "Everyone was smart, literate and opinionated. One guy could look at an IBM product announcement and explain how its pricing would unfold for the next three years. Another would talk about retail channel strategies and how they differed in the U.S. and France. The Japanese were coming out of their transistor radio phase and we puzzled over whether Fujitsu or Amdahl would be IBM's toughest competitor and who else would win – the computer companies that bought into telecommunications or the telcos that bought into computers. Gartner Group became the preferred place a corporate client went when it had any question about the IT industry."

"Everyone was important, down to the littlest guy," recalled another Gartnerite. "The feeling was that we were all connected, all working toward the same goal, and all willing to do whatever it took to get there."

Getting into Gartner Group

At a time when America was enthralled by the "Star Wars" movie series, Gartnerites saw themselves as Jedi warriors and Gideon as the Jedi Master. An alumnus said, "Gideon and his team did a phenomenal job of building a culture of intellectual pioneers, dedicated to protecting business consumers and monetizing their knowledge."

Top-notch talent became a byword for Gartner Group. In an interview with *MIT Management* magazine, Gideon was asked what he looked for in prospective hires. His reply: "Our analysts and account executives have most likely worked in the industry for ten to 15 years. Our analysts are supposed to be both intuitive and analytical. They must generate breakthrough ideas easily. They're known for giving clear and detailed and gutsy opinions, and then changing those opinions if the evidence changes. We have hired some people out of business school, but generally we hire experienced people. There is wisdom that comes only from having been a participant. Forecasting in the computer and communications industries requires a certain historical perspective.

"The people we bring in from the outside analyze and evaluate the marketplace and provide leadership to our clients. They focus full-time on what is going on in the industry. They spend all of their time trying to understand the economics of our business, who is doing what to whom in the marketplace, what the major issues are. They speak continuously with their peers, users, suppliers, venture capitalists, and financial sources. They are exposed to a breadth of information that is orders of magnitudes greater than they had at their disposal before they joined Gartner Group."

A job interview with Gideon rarely followed the expected format, as Ken Sonenclar discovered. To begin with, rather than meeting in Stamford, Gideon suggested that they get together for dinner the following Wednesday in Manhattan. (At the time, Sonenclar was living in the city, so he appreciated not having to travel to Stamford.) "Then Gideon hesitated for a moment," Sonenclar recalled. "I assumed he remembered some conflict and was about to pick a new date. Instead, he told me that the Boston Symphony was in town and that he had an extra ticket. Would I like to join him at Carnegie Hall? Like most people, I'm not used to symphony invitations from strangers, let alone as part of a job interview. 'Sure,' I said. 'Terrific!' Gideon chirped. 'Why don't you pick some place to eat beforehand. Just call my assistant.'"

Their dinner passed quickly with pleasant conversation about restaurants, movies and Gideon's recent ski trip. There was no mention of Gene Amdahl and his super-computer, IBM's System/38, mass storage or a college drop-out named Bill Gates who had recently been making headlines in the trade press. Before long, Gideon and Sonenclar were sinking into their red velvet seats at Carnegie Hall, just as Claudio Abbado picked up his baton to conduct Mahler. Gideon was enthralled, while Sonenclar was grateful just to stay awake. At the end of the evening, Gideon said encouragingly, "Don't give up on Mahler. He'll grow on you." Then he promised to be in touch.

That was the total course of the interview. Sonenclar soon joined the firm as the Programs Director.

The final step of the hiring process was a full-out gauntlet innocuously dubbed the group interview. These began with the prospective analyst being introduced and defending a piece of research that he/she had written. But within a few minutes, the meeting devolved into a rapid-fire, free-form inquisition with anywhere from five to eight Gartner analysts grilling the "new meat" on any related topic they could think of: Why is IBM failing in MRP II software? How would you contrast the MicroVAX against the System/38 in a manufacturing setting? What are the three most effective tools you can use to manage inventory?

"It was an improvisational dance of the mind," recalled Bill Keller. "But it was a very effective tool because it tested the true abilities and skills of the analysts-to-be. It showed how they could or could not control a crowd, lead the conversation, think on their feet, and sell, all at the same time."

Of course, these intellectual free-for-alls were also opportunities for senior analysts to show off their own smarts in front of their colleagues, a lure few could resist. Keller never forgot his own group interview interchange with senior analyst Bill McSpadden.

McSpadden demanded, "Name a relationship between an automobile manufacturer and a software company and tell me the significance."

"General Motors and Teknowledge," Keller promptly replied. "GM has a financial relationship in Teknowledge, which is expected to deliver advanced systems to selected GM assembly plants." He remembered feeling pretty smart.

"That is correct," Bill conceded. "But it's not the example I was thinking of. Try again!"

"Try again?!" Keller thought. "The right answer wasn't the right answer? This sucks." But he kept his cool and quickly blurted out, "Ford and American Cimflex. Ford is the largest customer of Cimflex, which is building proprietary software for its next-generation auto plants."

McFadden didn't say a word. Keller had passed the test.

Expect the Unexpected

Once in the fold, new hires found themselves in a workplace unlike any other. On Joel Wecksell's first day of work, he looked out of his office door and saw someone riding a bike down the hall, followed by a very small dog. When he dropped by another colleague's office, he found piles of suitcases and laundry from the colleague's officemate. Wecksell said, "It turned out he used the office to store his dirty laundry – and to this day, I still don't know why." But Wecksell knew one thing immediately: "This was going to be a place I would either love very much or hate." He stayed for 19 years.

At a time when formal dress codes were unquestioned and unwavering, Gartner Group's shunning of dress codes was seen by many as shocking. But at the firm, the sentiment was that if comfortable clothing helped produce good research, then jeans and T-shirts were okay.

On Stacey Hawkins' first day at Gartner, she was astonished by how many people popped into her office to introduce themselves and welcome her to the firm – including a guy wearing old sneakers, ragged blue jeans and a wrinkled orange T-shirt with a map of Africa emblazoned on the front. "I thought it was exceptionally nice that the janitor stopped in to say hello," Hawkins said. Of course, it was Peter Wright.

Wright wasn't the only analyst to take dressing down to new depths. Rob Goddu recalled an eye-opening meeting with the IT leadership team from Schering Plough. Gartner analyst Mike Braude was supposed to do a presentation on software scenarios but at the last minute was unable to attend. He sent Chris Bird as his substitute. Goddu described the scene: "Into the midst of this ultra-conservative group of businessmen all wearing suits and ties walked this large, pale guy sporting two to three days of unshaven growth on his face, white denim cutoff shorts, strings dangling and all, and a semi-transparent white linen button-down shirt with the sleeves cut off, strings dangling there as well. Leather flip-flops completed the ensemble. He looked like he'd been lost at sea for a week. There was a pregnant pause as Chris sat down – a few jaws almost hit the table." But in the end, Bird did a phenomenal job, the clients renewed their services – and thereafter, Gartner's sales team learned to dress business casual for future visits.

Why did Gideon allow such sloppy dress? He responded, "When I was at IBM, all males were forced to wear jacket and tie. So I thought I'd test whether dress made a difference. It sure didn't. In fact, many Gartnerites were proud of our 'Freedom of the dress.'"

Even so, precautionary memos would be distributed the day before a client was due to visit. "We all knew what that meant: Dress appropriately and do not smoke wacky weed in the hallways," Stacey Hawkins said. "Of course, the smell carried right out the doors of the offices...." Marijuana was used recreationally and generally tolerated at the firm. And just in case anyone got the munchies, the company cafeteria regularly set out bowls of fresh fruit and healthy fare.

Work hard/play hard was another key element of Gartner Group culture that sowed the seeds for the volleyball courts and Ping-

Pong tables that would dot Silicon Valley campuses in years to come. Every week at Gartner there was a TGIF (Thank God It's Friday) party for the entire company, held in the cafeteria. Everyone who was in the office stopped by for pizza, beer, wine and great conversation. Gideon's crew also organized an annual party on March 13th in honor of his birthday; the month following, the firm funded a blow-out bash to celebrate the anniversary of the company's founding. In fact, anyone's birthday was a good reason to unleash bottles of booze from the company storage cabinet, sparking informal parties.

"Our spouses, dates, and significant others never quite understood why we spent a huge amount of time socializing with the very same people whom we worked with for eight to twelve intense hours every day," Jonathan Yarmis remembered. "It was a magical time with a magical group of people. We worked very hard to build a great business but at the same time, we knew if we were going to work that hard, it had better be with a group of people we enjoyed being around. And believe me, after twenty-three kamikazes, we were *a lot* of fun to be around." So much fun, in fact, that many Gartnerites met their future spouses at work.

Creative Contentiousness

Research meetings, held regularly every Friday at lunch, were a unique feature of Gartner Group culture. *Creative Contentiousness* was the order of the day.

"Meetings were a combination of camaraderie and intense disagreement," David Familiant said. "Gideon believed that conflict created ideas. He wanted to make sure that everyone stood behind their conviction strongly enough to convince him. I've never seen a smarter group of people or people with stronger opinions who were not afraid to voice them. It was definitely not a 'yes, sir' kind of environment."

The format was simple: Between three and five analysts would each get up in turn and put out what Gideon called a "stalking horse," which, as mentioned, meant a preliminary analysis of a recent development. It was the focus and function of the group to comment on and challenge the analyst's point of view, as well as help them finalize their thinking. While the meetings could be the verbal equivalent of a blood sport, they were, in fact, a terrific opportunity for learning. Since the analyst reporting on the developments in his or her area of focus was challenged by the most critical audience possible – their colleagues, Gideon and Dave Stein – the presentation also served as a crash course in one or more aspects of the IT business, a public speaking challenge, and a great way to build company cohesiveness.

Watching colleagues eviscerate each other was too compelling to miss, both for the educational value and simply as a form of entertainment. No analyst was ever out of the office on a Friday. Unshaven, grungy analysts would stumble off the red-eye from the West Coast and into the office, just so that they could witness that week's flaying.

Erik Keller recalled a typical exchange during which he challenged his colleague and friend George Weiss, who covered Tandem Computer with regard to its long-term prospects. Erik pointed out that less than ten percent of Tandem's revenue came from the manufacturing sector, which made up over thirty percent of the world economy. Given that, how could Tandem survive?

George replied, "Erik, that's an excellent point. You know the manufacturing sector so well and no one would ever think to challenge you in this area."

"That's nice, George, but please stop sucking up to me and answer the question!"

George took the jibe in stride, Keller recalled, although he made up for it by wiping Keller off the court during their next tennis game. That, too, was typical. "You challenged someone's ideas around lunch and then bought him a beer at the Crab Shell after work," Keller said. "That's the way it was."

Challenging a colleague was commonplace. However, the way to truly earn respect at the research meeting was to be able to get Gideon, Dave Stein or Mike Braude, who often ran the meetings, to stand down and back off. Anyone who could achieve that rare accomplishment counted it as one of the highlights of their tenure at the firm.

Erik Keller remembered his moment of glory: In late 1990, IBM had just introduced a big marketing program into manufacturing called CIM (Computer Integrated Manufacturing) architecture. It included many hardware platforms and systems software. Keller was asked to deliver an analysis of the program and its prospects during one Friday research meeting. As a relatively young analyst still earning his research chops, he was more than a little nervous.

His findings stood at odds with IBM. Big Blue continued to push its traditional mainframe S/370 and mid-range AS/400 solutions to buyers, saying this was what buyers should select for manufacturing, whereas Gartner had written that the market would be purchasing PCs and Unix-based solutions regardless of company size or need. Keller went through Gartner's scenarios and why Gartner claimed PCs and Unix stations would grab the market rather than IBM's proposed solutions.

"As I was getting into my analysis," Keller recalled, "Mike Braude stood up and said, 'Well, I really don't understand why the AS/400 won't work. It's like any other computer.'

"I don't know what happened but I snapped, 'Mike, the AS/400 is not like any other computer. First of all, it can't compile C, at least not efficiently, and that's the language every new application is being written in today. Second, it can't effectively run floating point or scientific operations, making it inappropriate for lots of manufacturing applications. And third, it lacks key integration and networking mechanisms to attach to shop-floor controllers and distributed control systems. Now please sit down and let me finish!'"

To his amazement, Mike did – and the others erupted into cheers. Keller had faced down Braude and lived to tell the tale.

"But this was simply just one part of the culture and exercise," Keller continued. "Mike wasn't being a jerk – even though that's what many people often thought. He was just making sure you knew your stuff and could defend your ideas and concepts. And that's what our Friday research meetings were all about."

Life with Gideon

Above all, there was Gideon, adding style – "Everyone else is in jeans and here he is wearing Armani before any of us knew who Armani was," recalled administrative assistant Karen Pierce, "Gideon was always coming up with seemingly crazy ideas that turned out to be seeds of genius, and making sure that life at Gartner Group would never be dull.

"What I enjoyed about working at Gartner was the challenge of working directly with Gideon," David Familiant said. "You never really knew from one day to the next what would be on his mind, and that made things interesting."

Gideon conceded that he probably created turmoil, especially when his ideas were the boat-rocking, feather-ruffling kind they often were. Some people, especially those bred to more conventional working environments, found Gideon too "spur of the moment." One employee, formerly a 25-year IBM man, complained, "You could have a plan in place and then he might come in one day with a new idea." Not surprisingly, the IBM-er didn't last at Gartner. But others thrived in the maelstrom. Peter Wright said, "Gideon creates turmoil because people don't like change, and he always wants to create a better mousetrap."

Stories about Gideon abounded.

"Gideon introduced me as the newest employee and gave me that year's holiday present – a cordless phone," recalled Karen Pierce. "He said he decided to give everyone a cordless phone because he had tried to call an analyst and couldn't reach him because the analyst was on the toilet. He then laughingly told that there were no longer excuses for not taking his calls at home!"

Gideon was very closely involved in all aspects of the company on a daily basis. As many typical entrepreneurs do, he was always thinking up different ways to organize and reorganize functional areas and always coming up with new ideas and schemes. "Many of the senior management team dreaded Monday mornings because Gideon had the whole weekend to come up with a new list of ideas and suggestions," recalled Dorothy Langer, the first head of Marketing and Sales. "One of Gideon's minor ideas was that the sales department should have a bell, which would be rung whenever a salesperson brought in new business, and it should be loud enough for everyone in the building – at the time, on Soundview Avenue – to hear it. My sales guys thought it was a kooky idea, but we installed the bell. It turned out to be a great morale booster for all of the employees and especially for my sales team."

Another time, Gideon was complaining during a meeting that analysts took too long to write research notes. To illustrate his point, he composed one during the meeting – in fifteen minutes.

He was a master showman in front of an audience – although he occasionally allowed himself the luxury of a smidgen of stage fright. Mike Schumer's favorite anecdote about Gideon involved him being invited to give a speech at the annual meeting of the National Telecommunications Association in Dallas. This was quite a coup, since the speech was to be given to an elite group – the organization's executive committee, consisting of about sixty people who were the bosses of the telecom managers in Fortune 500 companies. (At the time, the term "Chief Information Officer" had not been coined, but these were the people who typically became the CIOs of their companies.)

Schumer recalled, "When Gideon found that he was to give the speech, he became very agitated and sent me a note saying something like, 'I cannot give this speech. I know nothing about telecom. Who does Stanley Cohen (our telecom specialist, hired from Yankee Group, who had arranged for Gideon to give the speech) think I am – "bleeping" Howard Anderson (the head of Yankee Group)? Please meet with me to help me with the speech.' So I met with Gideon and reminded him that the people he would be speaking to were really IT people and that he had a lot in common with them. But that did not seem to impress him. He continued to say that he knew nothing about telecom, that the speech would be a 'bleeping' disaster."

Gideon and Schumer arrived in Dallas the night before the speech and, after checking into the hotel, met to discuss a few ideas about the exponential growth of data networking. They finished around midnight and Gideon predicted that he'd be up all night writing and rewriting the speech, all the while lamenting what a disaster it would be.

The next morning, Gideon and Schumer were invited to have breakfast with the conference participants. Gideon demurred, telling Schumer that he was worried sick about the speech.

At 8:30 a.m., Gideon was introduced. After the applause died down, he began his presentation. Schumer recalled, "In his inimitable fashion, he created a stalking horse for the growth of computer networking, using his trademark method of making reasonable assumptions and creating a spread-sheet which analyzed data communications growth and its financial implications. This was the very combination of industry knowledge and financial acumen that made Gartner Group successful, and the audience was mesmerized. After the speech, they swarmed around Gideon like ants on a cookie crumb. He finally broke loose and as we walked away from the meeting, I said, 'Gideon, that was wonderful!' And he replied, 'Why? Haven't you ever heard me speak before?'"

"I never tried to do anything that wasn't unique," Gideon said. "We had many innovations at our conferences."

From the start, Gartner Group conferences set their own pattern. At the time, virtually every conference in the technology field featured outside speakers – journalists, technology experts or company executives, each with his or her point of view and agenda. Gartner Group conferences might invite one outsider to serve as keynote speaker but every other "name" was followed by a title that included the words "Gartner Group." It was a way to demonstrate the expertise that ran so broadly and deeply throughout the firm, as well as to ensure that the information being shared was completely non-biased. "We were pitching objectivity," Gideon explained, and the conferences amplified that message, over and over.

Gartner's first conference in 1979 was attended by forty-five people. Karen Healy, who built many Gartner conferences and rose from Gideon's assistant to Senior Vice President, recalled, "We worked all night the day before, with everyone, including Gideon and Dave Stein, collating the materials in a hotel room, then de-collating them because one of the presentations had to include a minor change!"

Gartner's second conference was held at the Concord Hotel in the Catskills, an immense establishment that had once been the epitome of Borscht Belt palaces. Because the Concord was a strictly kosher establishment, there were two separate kitchens and two separate dining rooms. Meals were family style and the amount of food was immense enough to make the tables buckle. The event went very well, Karen Healy remembered, with 125 attendees, including clients Dick Imershein from IBM and Noel Zakin from AT&T, both of whom later joined the Gartner staff. The highlight was the featured speaker Lester Thurow, a famous economist, author and dean of the Sloan School of Management at MIT, who was a personal acquaintance of Gideon. Karen Healy recalled, "The audience was transfixed by his summary of the world's economies, although it had little to do with technology."

At its very beginning, Gartner Group offered only one service focused on a variety of information services (called IS), and the firm held just one annual conference. "As we sliced and diced the pie into more and more services, we added more and more conferences, since every service director wanted his/her own conference," Karen Healy said. "We got up to as many as twenty-four in a year, not to mention many regional user meetings, sales meetings and other events that could be slipped in under the radar."

Obviously, this wasn't a sustainable model. Gideon soon came up with yet another innovative idea: an annual get-together known as the Scenario Conference. The scenarios followed a particular format: Each scenario was presented by the appropriate service head, who described the qualitative and quantitative macro trends of the sector as a whole. This was followed by presentations of the key issues Gartner Group analysts predicted their clients would face, such as projections of overall and sub-sector growth, the competitive challenges to be confronted, new technologies coming into the pipeline, and so on. "Everything we wrote ultimately related to a key issue or to the scenario," Gideon explained. "The point was to create a standard structure which clients could get used to and grow to love, which I believe they did."

"*Conference prep* were the two scariest words in all of Gartnerdom," recalled Jonathan Yarmis. "There were always several deadlines, each with increasing levels of reality and urgency. As the real deadline approached, we were, of course, always down to the last minute, which meant all-nighters, sometimes even sleeping in the office. Usually around 7 p.m. on those nights, a group of us would head out for burgers and beers at Tumbledown's in Riverside to fuel up for the marathon."

One thing that disconcerted analysts who joined Gartner from large, mature organizations such as AT&T or IBM, was the relatively small number of support staff. A mere baker's dozen of employees pulled off 30-plus conferences annually. Gartner Group analysts were expected to stuff binders; wives, husbands and friends were encouraged to pitch in, too. With personal attention a premium element of the firm, each analyst was assigned to host a table of clients at lunch but Mike Schumer recalled that at one conference, the staffing was so low that his wife Carole was called on to host a table of clients on her own. She was such a hit, Mike noted, "at subsequent conferences, these clients expected to be seated with her and were disappointed if she didn't join me at the conference."

By the end of the 1980s, the burgeoning number of conferences had been pruned down to a handful of "theme" conferences with representation from all services. The flagship event was – and continues to be – Symposium/L.C.Xpo.

Kathy Foreman Kane remembered sitting with her colleagues in the events group at a glass conference table in Gideon's corner office on the second floor of 56 Top Gallant Road in early 1988. Gideon entered carrying a sheaf of loose papers and a thick book. He threw them on the table and said, "This is what I want to do for the IT industry." The book was a program guide from the World Economic Forum, which Gideon had just attended in Davos, Switzerland; the papers were his design for a defining new Gartner event. "Gideon wanted to create an event that would have as much impact on the IT industry as the World Economic Forum had on the world," Kathy recalled. "This is how the Gartner Symposium was born."

The East and West Coast Scenario Conferences were merged into one week-long conference, held that October at the Dolphin Hotel at Walt Disney World. Over 1,200 people registered.

"There were multiple tracks, so people could create their own agenda," Karen Healy explained. "Our clients could schedule personal consultations with analysts. And since we had a huge captive audience of technology buyers, the Symposium was a prime market for all the industry manufacturers, whom we convinced to host a trade show." The Gartner difference: All the booths were the same size and manufacturers were limited to buying only two booths. Even IBM could buy no more space than a tiny vendor with only 20 clients. "No one manufacturer could own the show," Karen noted. "That was a way for us to remain impartial and not look as though we were biased toward one vendor." The first Symposium trade show was so successful that, Karen recalled, "every vendor wanted to be there." It not only enhanced Gideon's concept of synergy, but became a huge boost to the firm's bottom line.

"Little did I know at that time that I was part of something big that would become a true 'industry-defining' event and would carry so much clout that it would bring in luminaries such as Bill Gates, Scott McNealy, Lou Gerstner and many, many others," Kathy Foreman Kane reminisced. "That at its height, it would attract over 13,000 participants and bring in over 500 exhibitors. That it would become an international brand with events in Japan, Australia, France, Spain, South Africa and other locations. That it would build a community of over 30,000 people every year. But I think the best part of it all was the camaraderie the event inspired within Gartner. The entire company came together to produce this event. It was Gartner Group at its best."

"When Gideon came back from Davos and announced, 'We're going to create our own Davos,' we all thought he was nuts," David

Familiant recalled. "Today, it's huge – absolutely the conference of the IT industry." The creation, development and success of the Symposium was, he said, pure Gideon. "From one small idea that everyone thinks is nuts, he makes it happen."

The Gartner Touch

In addition to hosting its one-of-a-kind conferences, Gartner Group put its own distinctive panache on other people's conferences as a way to further differentiate itself to clients and prospects. Almost everyone affiliated with the firm during the mid-1980s remembers how Gideon revamped the firm's approach to CeBIT in 1986.

Held in Hanover, Germany, at the world's largest fairground, CeBIT was the world's largest computer exposition in the mid-80s. (CeBIT is a German acronym that translates to *Center for Office Automation, Information Technology and Telecommunication*.) At events of this magnitude, it's almost a given that visitors get lost and exhausted on the exposition floor. They trudge through miles of aisles, wasting huge amounts of time stopping at many booths that really have little relevance to their interests. Even if they are lucky enough to stumble upon the right booth, they often have to fight the crowds on the floor (with little access, if any, to the exhibiting company's executives).

Bill Rosser recalled: "Gideon had already visited CeBIT in 1985 and decided to design a new approach whereby we could invite our best clients and prospects to join us there and offer a service that would knock their socks off, thus maximizing our market impact and strengthening our relationship."

While Gartner, together with most other companies, hosted its clients at parties – Gideon oversaw and guided the firm's clients' entire experience at CeBIT, 24/7. Gideon explained: "I asked each of several Gartner analysts to arrive an entire day or two before the opening and I arranged with CeBIT to allow our analysts to canvass the huge floor while companies were finishing building their booths. It was over 250,000 square feet with more than 3,000 exhibitors, and we used this opportunity to find the five or ten firms which would be *most* relevant to the issues being faced by each of our invited U.S. clients who were senior executives at their firms. The most major booths at CeBIT are, huge two-level indoor structures where their product demos would be on the ground level, with fancy refreshments served upstairs (invariably by young and attractive European ladies). Chosen visitors were invited to meet with executives of the firms in private conference rooms. Luckily, since we were by then a very influential advisory firm in the IT space, our team obtained prior and private access to the senior executives of these firms. This way, we were able to set up specific appointments for our clients during the exposition. It was a luxury."

"I was one of the worker bees," Bill Rosser said. "My job, along with Chuck White, was to scour the whole fairgrounds to find the latest and most interesting new products and developments in several key areas where we had expertise and representation at the show. We set up a schedule so that at designated times, the senior representative at the booth could greet and answer questions from our group. We had three working analysts with us, so we set up three 'tours.' Furthermore, Chuck and I wrote and distributed a daily 'scoop sheet' which revealed the hot stuff and built even more interest among our clients and prospects." After chaperoning his or her five invited clients through the itinerary, from selected exhibit to selected exhibit, each Gartner analyst then recapped and discussed the day's experience. "This was a breath of fresh air and everybody loved it," Rosser said.

Being given a customized guided tour of the latest technology was fun and exciting, but the Gartner special touch didn't stop there. "Off the trade grounds – wow!" Rosser recalled. "Our guest clients were invited to stay in a gorgeous old castle done up with modern conveniences. It was not really near the fairgrounds, but no problem! Gartner Group arranged a helicopter to pick up our guests at the castle, lift them over the rooftops and deposit them on a landing pad in the middle of the fairgrounds – and, of course, return them to the castle at the end of the day. And just to make sure the clients would be paying attention, when cocktail hour was held at the castle, we brought in 'ringers.' I remember Bill Caffery (one of our top analysts) standing halfway up a spiral staircase leading up from the castle forecourt and giving a 15-minute speech. It was marvelous.

"To me, that was Gartner," Rosser concluded. "Taking a new spin, trying out remarkable new concepts, focusing on pleasing the clients, building new relationships."

What Gideon designed was unique: obtaining pre-fair access to the very senior executives of major technology firms, negotiating private sessions between those executives and our senior U.S. clients, and taking care of those clients to the nth degree.

Going Public

By the mid-1980s, Gartner Group literature stated, "The industry has accorded Gartner Group recognition as the most respected, value-added information provider to information systems suppliers." An article in *MIT Management* elaborated, "Every day, in myriad ways, Gartner Group analysts support ... decisions that are made by the men and women who annually spend ... hundreds of billions of dollars buying [and designing and investing in] large and medium-size computer systems, personal computers, workstations, peripherals, systems and applications software, office products and communications transmission equipment."

Or as Gideon put it succinctly: "We are the source for all data processing- and telecommunication-related decisions that large organizations make."

With revenues surging year over year, Gartner Group had edged into profitability in the fourth quarter of 1984, and by 1985 was solidly in the black. That precipitated a crucial decision. Gideon explained, "When you have venture capitalists in the act, you know that your future is either the sale of the company or a public offering because the VCs eventually liquidate or liquefy their investment. So it was inevitable that at some point Gartner Group would go public."

Gartner Group always seemed to be in expansion mode. Gideon said: "We wanted to expand our international presence and felt that even though we had a sizable sales organization, it was still not providing the coverage that we really wanted." That was one reason for going public. Another reason: "We didn't have any capital (except for stock) to do strategic acquisitions. We had completed two small ones before 1986 and felt that perhaps we ought to consider doing others, in which case we should have some cash available." If Gartner wanted to expand, at some point it would need capital and floating an offering of public stock is generally the cheapest way to raise capital.

In July 1986, the company that had been founded seven years earlier with $675,000 in venture capital held an initial public offering of four million shares, priced at $10.50 per share. The IPO was wildly successful, raising about $11 million — $4 million for the company and just under $7 million to selling stockholders. Although some key Gartner employees became instant millionaires, it's worth noting that none of the selling shareholders sold more than 25 percent of their stock. They were confident that the company would continue to grow and prosper.

Gartner Group had been founded as a three-legged stool, selling information to technology vendors, technology users and institutional investors. While most of its resources were devoted to the first two areas, some at Gartner, led by Peter Wright, believed that what had essentially been a department had the potential to become a substantial Wall Street brokerage including a full trading department, stronger sales resources and ultimately money management and even corporate finance. Gideon recalled, "I loved that kind of get-up-and-go, and we were already beginning to sell to venture capital firms and were tinkering with other opportunities. But we had neither the capital nor manpower at the time to be aggressive. Plus my own plate was very full."

When a Gartner Initial Public Offering ("IPO") was first considered, the firm's board of directors pointed out an obvious hitch: The Wall Street model for calculating profit and loss (P&L) was so different from the Gartner model that potential Gartner IPO investors would be confused. The board's suggestion was to spin out the brokerage business. Gideon concurred, and by late 1985, soon before Gartner went public, Gartner Securities was spun out and became a separate company.

Peter Wright, one of the biggest proponents of the spin-off, was named president of the newly independent firm. He was joined by outside analysts as well as seasoned pros who transferred from Gartner with Gideon's blessing. They were all excited by the potential to develop an investment bank that specialized in the exciting, fast-growing info-tech industry and could draw on a rich resource that no other investment house had: the proven quality of Gartner Group research.

Gartner Securities was renamed Soundview Financial Group after the sale of Gartner Group to Saatchi & Saatchi to avoid the confusion of too many companies with the Gartner name. Soundview was unique in that it combined accepted Wall Street research and distribution methods, with a close, albeit "arms length", relationship with Gartner analysts. It became the leading technology research boutique on Wall Street. The company was acquired by Charles Schwab in 2003.

Gideon's New Roles

As the firm grew, Gideon had little time for his original role as primary analyst. He focused on running the company, directing its future course, and constantly coming up with creative ideas for continued growth. At the same time, he took on other responsibilities that expanded his horizons, specifically teaching. It gave him great satisfaction, both personally and professionally.

For example, at Gartner, Gideon created and presented a course every year to the entire research department that refreshed old hands and trained new hires in what was now known as the Gartner style of research – a combination of deep thinking, hard facts, strong opinions and a certain flair that imbued everything from writing to presentations.

In addition, he also taught a course for second-year students at UCLA's Anderson School of Management, an experience that he called "my most satisfying professional achievement." Gideon recalled, "I already had some dealings with a senior professor at the school. In scanning the course directory, I found several computer-oriented courses but I also sensed a large gap between theory and practice – in other words, lots of theory and little practice! Without considering how much work would be involved, I asked Professor Ephraim "Eph" McLean who led the university's graduate IT practice if there were some way I could impose myself into the UCLA system and teach a course on the structure of the technology industry, which my company was already deeply involved in analyzing for corporate clients. The answer was 'Yes!'"

Gideon set about designing a new course for second-year students at this major institution. "I was totally unprepared for the caliber of the students," Gideon recalled. "They almost universally had some experience in the computer industry. In other words, they did not go from undergraduates to graduate school but had work experience in the computer field, so they were quite knowledgeable. Because each one had different experiences, their knowledge was quite diverse. They were also very outspoken, which made them great fun to work with."

The subject of the course was the structure of the computer industry. Gideon gave the first two and final lecture and brought senior analysts from Gartner Group to prepare and contribute knowledge other lectures in their area of expertise, such as the software or minicomputer sector. "I would introduce them, they would speak for about an hour, and then I moderated and contributed to a free-form discussion, with my summary at the end," Gideon said. He usually assigned demanding projects to the students and despite his crammed calendar, personally graded them and then discussed them one-on-one. The course was a breath of fresh air for the students, as its design was based on real-world experiences with contributions from actual practitioners instead of traditional faculty.

Student response was off the charts. The course was unanimously voted the best course that the students took at UCLA Graduate School of Management throughout their two years of study.

Gideon found a way to combine work and pleasure to make an onerous weekly cross-country commute into a fun experience. The class was held from 9 a.m. to noon on Mondays. Gideon would fly out to Los Angeles on Sunday and stay on campus, at the Anderson School's accommodations for visiting faculty. A friend happened to be attending the business school, and after lunch, they'd play tennis for a few hours in the Southern California sunshine. Then Gideon would catch the 4 o'clock afternoon flight back to New York.

An Unexpected Success

Steve Zucker, who became Gartner Group's Controller, originally met Gideon in Steve's capacity as a manager of Oppenheimer's accounting firm, which Gideon had hired to audit financial reports and prepare tax returns when he founded Gartner Group. At their first meeting, Gideon laid out his five-year projections for the not-yet-born business. In what would turn out to be a phrase repeated over and over, not just by Zucker, but by just about everyone associated with the firm, Zucker said, "I thought his projections would be difficult to achieve but they turned out to be too conservative."

Companies almost always reflect the personalities and skill sets of the founder and Gartner Group was no exception. Bob Fleming, who joined the firm in May 1983, fresh out of Wharton Business School, remarked, "One of Gideon's great strengths and, ultimately, one of the company's strengths as well, was his ability to take multiple disparate pieces of information, often seemingly unrelated, and put them together to draw meaningful conclusions that had our clients wondering why they hadn't thought of them. In a sense, that was the story behind the company. Yes, there were other IT consulting shops at the time, like Yankee Group and Dataquest, but none had demonstrated that their business could scale beyond $10 million. Gartner took elements of its business model from many sources and became critical to its clients' success – and its own."

By the late 1980s, the IT industry was no longer an arcane collection of geeks. It was the cool place to work, the next big thing, and everyone wanted to be a part of it.

"Whenever people outside the office found out I worked at Gartner, I could see the envy in their eyes," Peggy Pedwano recalled. Her favorite memory of her time at Gartner involved an incident on the commuter train from New York to Stamford. The train car was full and Pedwano hadn't been able to get a seat, so she was standing in the crowded vestibule by the door. "People were chatting the way they do on their commute and someone asked me where I worked. When I said, 'Gartner,' the whole crowd went silent. They all wanted to hear what I had to say. It was a great feeling."

one of the many Gartner outings

Gideon and his team, strategizing

Chapter 11: Second Thoughts

The initial public offering of Gartner Group in 1986 marked yet another milestone in the company's record of innovations: It was the first data analysis company to do so – and the result was stunningly successful. At the same time, the firm was racking up other achievements: *Business Week* ranked it ninth on its 1987 list of "Best Small Companies and Corporations." An overwhelming majority of the top Fortune 100 companies were now committed Gartner clients.

It would seem that the firm's future was assured. Precisely because the prognosis was so positive, it was the perfect time to consider selling the company.

Selling Gartner Group had been in the cards ever since the company's inception. Gideon also had personal reasons for selling: "Having been raised in a middle-class milieu, I was motivated to sell out at some point," he explained. "My family was larger. I needed capital."

It wasn't as if there hadn't been nibbles from prospective buyers. In fact, during the 1980s, there were plenty of firms that were interested in buying Gartner. "We always listened," Gideon said. "I was always interested in knowing what our value was in the market."

Gideon traveled to London and to the Netherlands. "Three different publishing companies there were after us," he recalled. In addition, "Dun & Bradstreet was after us. Prentice Hall was after us."

In Gartner Group, publishing companies saw a firm that had created a new, sexy and wildly successful sector in a traditionally staid industry, and they all wanted to own some of that magic. Gideon noted, "I think they saw that we were a publishing firm, too. After all, we produced a huge amount of paper, especially when we went to the single-page research sheet format. We produced a lot more than organizations that published long reports, because you can knock off a page in two hours, whereas when you have to write a 10-page, or 25-page or 50-page document, it becomes so psychologically defeating to even think about completing it that it takes you forever. We were much more productive when coming out with two-pagers, and since every analyst at Gartner Group was producing these notes, we produced a lot of them."

Gideon continued, "So we spoke to these publishing firms. But the terms never seemed right for us and for a while, we did nothing."

Sometimes the match didn't go anywhere because the personalities of the people at the top didn't click. Neill Brownstein, whose Bessemer Venture Partners had been one of the two original investors, remembers what sank the hopes of one prospective buyer, the head of a publishing company who wanted to hire Gideon as part of the deal. "We all went to the Metropolitan Opera. The

CEO of the publishing company fell asleep – and it wasn't an opera that would ordinarily put you to sleep. Gideon said, 'I'm not going to sell my company to this guy. If he falls asleep at the opera, I don't want to work for him!'"

Meanwhile, the financial frenzy of the 1980s was reaching its zenith. A five-year bull market had seen the Dow Jones Industrial Average (DJIA) rise from 776 points in August 1982 to a high of 2,722 points in August 1987.

Then came Black Monday, October 19, 1987, when the bottom dropped out of stock markets around the world. The Dow dropped by 508 points to 1,738.74, a sickening slump of 22.61 percent, and the largest one-day percentage drop in its history. The S&P 500 was similarly affected, sliding over 20 percent. $500 billion vaporized overnight. Gartner Group's stock price was caught in the maelstrom and plunged precipitously.

Many people feared that a major recession would result. Gideon was among them. "Believing that a major recession was in the offing, I decided to accelerate our efforts to sell the company," Gideon said. A Gartner employee had contacts with Saatchi & Saatchi. A meeting was arranged, which led to a subsequent get-together. It looked as though Gartner had found a match.

The Saatchi & Saatchi Story

Saatchi & Saatchi, now a global advertising agency, was founded by brothers Maurice and Charles Saatchi in London in 1970. From the beginning, the agency was known for producing breakthrough edgy ads for clients ranging from British Airways to the Conservative Party. The firm's "Labour Isn't Working" campaign before the 1979 elections helped sweep Margaret Thatcher into power.

By 1974, Saatchi & Saatchi had built a reputation as London's "creative agency" — a small shop that turned out clever work. At that point, they were Britain's thirteenth-largest advertising agency. Not bad for a company that had only opened its doors in 1970, but small stuff for two brothers entertaining visions of conquering the global market.

From the moment they set up shop, the Saatchi brothers set upon an intense course of business acquisitions. Their dreams were on the grand scale: The brothers had no qualms about contacting agencies – many of which were substantially larger than theirs – and asking if they might want to be acquired by Saatchi & Saatchi. Most of the executives contacted by the Saatchis laughed off these buyout overtures as delusions of grandeur, but the brothers knew exactly what they were doing.

Nobody was laughing in 1975 when the Saatchis engineered a reverse takeover of Compton Partners – a stodgy, publicly traded London advertising company owned by New York's Compton Advertising. Compton had hoped to acquire Saatchi & Saatchi and install the brothers as the energetic, inventive management team which the older company needed to revive itself.

"Better yet," said the brothers, "in exchange for our talents, let us acquire you."

When the dust settled, the Saatchis had taken over a company twice as big as their own. Their unlikely catch included a majority share of the merged company's equity, a jackpot of blue-chip accounts like Procter & Gamble, and Compton's stock exchange listing. The newly combined company then ranked fourth in the UK.

The Compton coup established the pattern for future Saatchi acquisitions. The brothers' ultimate aim was to become the largest advertising agency in the world. To do that, however, Saatchi would have to go public. And to do that, it would need the support of The City, London's version of Wall Street, in order to obtain the necessary financing.

Maurice Saatchi and his financial officer Martin Sorrell devised a management system that monitored the company's financial condition daily and imposed rigid budgets on its ever-expanding roster of acquisitions. This system made a strong impression on the City's financiers. They provided the capital that made Saatchi & Saatchi London's top glamour stock and enabled the agency to launch the biggest acquisition binge the world of advertising has ever seen.

Along the way, Saatchi & Saatchi evolved from just an advertising company to a full-service, one-stop communications agency, offering clients not only advertising, but public relations, research, even legal and financial services.

In 1985, the Saatchis were buying companies, most of them American, at the rate of one a month. In 1986, the Saatchis capped their unprecedented corporate buying spree by paying $100 million for the New York-based Backer & Spielvogel, the largest sum ever paid for an ad agency. Weeks later, they smashed that record by paying nearly $500 million for Ted Bates Worldwide, the third largest agency in the United States.

With the Bates acquisition, the brothers had realized their dream. Saatchi & Saatchi was by far the largest advertising conglomerate in the world, operating on five continents and servicing more than fifty of the world's 100 largest companies. In addition to advertising agencies, the Saatchi & Saatchi juggernaut had begun to swallow up firms such as Peterson & Co. (trial litigation advisors), Cleveland Consulting (a management consulting group), and Hay Group (a personnel consulting firm).

In 1987, Saatchi set its sights on Gartner Group.

The Seduction of Synergy

In the wake of the 1987 stock market crash, Saatchi had retained Booz Allen, a top consulting firm, to strategize on how to regain growth. Its conclusion was that the consulting business was ripe for consolidation and that Saatchi could and should be the first to exploit this huge opportunity, which would be enhanced by many and various advantageous synergies. After all, the Saatchi conglomerate certainly had experience when it came to acquisition binges. Saatchi promptly acquired eleven firms in disparate areas of consulting in barely six months. Gartner Group, its first acquisition in the information technology space, capped off the list.

It seemed like a good idea at the time.

Gideon recalled, "Saatchi was trying to do with business-to-business consulting what it had done in advertising. By consolidating the consulting companies they had acquired with a main office, which focused on synergy opportunities, it could build a very interesting business. We were a growth company with a strong reputation and momentum in the hottest part of the consulting field. So we were the jewel and Saatchi really wanted us."

The Gartner acquisition followed Saatchi & Saatchi's strategy of acquiring small to mid-size companies that were strong in their niche. Saatchi would benefit from Gartner's in-depth knowledge of the computer industry, in order to make wise decisions regarding future acquisitions.

Gartner Group thought it would benefit from the deal because its potential new owner was theoretically able to offer the still-growing company any necessary capital support, as well as help the consulting firm increase market share on an international level.

Gideon met with a few of the CEOs of the companies Saatchi had acquired. His due diligence didn't discover any flaws. But Gideon still had doubts. "I was skeptical about Saatchi's stated objective of becoming the world's leading consultancy because it would still be an uphill fight with organizations like Arthur Andersen and others around. I felt that Gartner would be good for Saatchi but was not convinced that the converse would be true."

But Gartner's board of directors, with its preponderance of venture capitalists, saw the prospect of a handsome liquidity opportunity. And after working nonstop for so many years to create and develop the firm, Gideon himself was drawn to the possibility of retiring to his vacation home in Aspen, Colorado.

A deal was struck. On June 18, 1988, *The New York Times* announced, "Saatchi & Saatchi Holdings and the Gartner Group said yesterday that they had entered into an agreement for a Saatchi subsidiary to pay $22.50 a share, or $90.3 million, for the computer research company."

The amount was four times Gartner's annual revenue. Gartner's share price promptly soared $4.25 in over-the-counter trading.

The agreement stipulated that no major changes would be made within Gartner Group following the takeover. Business would proceed as usual for both entities, with Saatchi & Saatchi now acting as a holding company. Gideon would remain as chief executive for just under three years, until the end of the fiscal year in March 1992. On top of the purchase price, Saatchi put up a cash fund, which became a bonus fund for Gartner employees, so all of the employee shareholders were paid off.

Even so, the marriage was nearly annulled before consummation. All of the parties were assembled at the altar – in this case, the lawyers' offices. It was 4 a.m., Neill Brownstein recalled. "All of the real terms had been settled and the lawyers were negotiating the fine points, when Gideon said, 'I'm not going to sell this company.'"

The room went silent. No one could believe that literally minutes from signing the agreement, the whole thing could blow up. Before anyone could explode, Fred Frank, one of the lawyers spoke up. A gentlemanly fellow who never lost his temper and was, Brownstein said, "always the epitome of someone who was there to make things happen, not to fight anyone," Frank was still immaculately attired when everyone else's suits were wrinkled and their ties unknotted. "Gideon," he said gently, "this is forty times earnings. You're not going to see this again. Sign."

Gideon signed.

In retrospect, Brownstein said, "It was a dumb sale. We were doing fine. Warburg didn't have a need to sell it. Bessemer didn't have a need to sell it. I don't know why we sold it." He recalled a scene from the movie "Heaven Can Wait" in which the owner of the Los Angeles Rams, having just sold the football team, is sitting in the stands regretting his actions. His lawyer asks, "Why did you sell?" The former owner replies, "They offered me a big price."

The company that had been founded not even a decade earlier with an investment of $675,000 was now being offered $90.3 million – an unimaginable premium. As Brownstein explained, "We were just flabbergasted that anyone would pay that, so we said yes. We had public shareholders, after all, and some lawyer told us that we would not have been doing the right thing for our shareholders if we hadn't sold. Better we should have fired that lawyer. It was bad advice."

For some people, the sale signaled the end of Gartner Group. But others knew better. Peter Wright predicted, "Gideon will keep starting new businesses until the day he's in his coffin, and maybe even after." Anyone who knew Gideon knew he wouldn't retire quietly to Aspen. They knew they'd be hearing from him.

Jonathan Art

Chapter 12: The Buyback

On June 13, 1989, Gideon received a call to attend an emergency meeting of the CEOs of the eleven consulting firms Saatchi & Saatchi had acquired in its attempt to diversify from its advertising heritage. Sitting in one corner of the meeting room was Steve Schwartzman, CEO of Blackstone. He had some startling news: With Saatchi's stock tumbling on the London and New York stock exchanges, Saatchi was under pressure to divest itself of all eleven consultancies. Only eight months after buying Gartner Group, Saatchi was putting it on the auction block, with Blackstone as its auctioneer.

Steve said that the preferred route would be to sell all the consulting companies to one buyer. Gideon knew Steve from earlier days and, after overcoming his shock at the news, approached Steve. "I told him I personally and strongly felt that Gartner should not be sold to another firm," Gideon recalled. Based on his poor experience with Saatchi, Gideon felt that any larger IT- related publishing or consulting company would destroy Gartner's unique and intense culture. Gideon was convinced that Gartner Group should be an independent employee-owned company.

Gideon asked Steve if Gartner could put together a proposal to buy itself back with whatever financing they could muster. The CEO replied that at this point such a leveraged buy-out (LBO) would be considered a spoiler, and for the moment there would be no discussions allowed between potential buyers and the managements of the consultancies!

Gideon was distraught. As the CEO of a Saatchi-owned company, he was supposed to follow orders. He recalls the moment of anguish: "This had been my baby. I hated seeing what Saatchi had done with it, and couldn't bear the thought of watching my firm's further decline under the ownership of another company." Over a period of several weeks of hard thinking, Gideon decided to work with Saatchi according to the letter of his obligations – but as to the spirit of these same obligations, he decided to walk the fine line of resisting Saatchi's strategy, while simultaneously designing an alternative solution in which Saatchi would get the money it needed and Gartner would regain its independence.

First Steps

On the train returning home, Gideon listed some potential partners Gartner might consider in obtaining a possible LBO, including Welsh Carson, Shearson's LBO group, and both Warburg Pincus and Bessemer Venture Partners, which had provided the seed money to capitalize Gartner Group.

He soon met with Gartner financial advisor Jon Art. Together they began to re-analyze both Gartner's strengths and challenges. Ironically, they had never catalogued the firm's issues this rigorously. There was a feeling that any continued avoidance would lead to unavoidable future dislocations.

In Gideon's opinion, Gartner had suffered under Saatchi, but to the outside observer, the firm would ultimately still appear highly attractive. It continued to dominate its market with rapidly growing recurring revenue, as promoted. Yet Gideon worried that this image might not survive the due diligence of meticulous buyers.

At his request, Gartner's staff presented a comprehensive list of the challenges facing its continued business. Jon Art wrote a memo that was brutally critical, basing his opinion on the idea that the team seemed more suited to the entrepreneurial high-growth phase of the firm's early development, while lacking the professional experience to grow the business over $100 million. It was true that, with the exception of Gartner's vice-president of international sales, not a single one of the executives had significant management or P&L experience. Also, the firm had no COO and was suffering from a lack of operating executives who could effectively institute any required procedures and controls. Ironically, Gideon had recently reminded Saatchi that with his full-time CEO contract soon to expire, hiring another executive should be a number one priority. However, to meet its own highly aggressive earnings plan, Saatchi disallowed the acquisition of an expensive COO in both 1989 and 1990, while simultaneously deferring any improvements to Gartner's infrastructure.

As the month approached its close, Gideon again met with Schwartzman. "I told him our business would perform twice as well as an independent entity rather than being captive." Gideon remembered, "I also initiated a discussion of possibly breaking the company up, selling certain pieces of it while leaving its core to our people."

Steve Schwartzman had his hands full dealing with the entire consulting group and had little patience for the argument. He insisted Gartner should be sold whole, expeditiously, and for a reasonable sum. Gideon didn't hide that he was now arguing on behalf of Gartner, not Saatchi. "I repeated that if we sold to a third party I'd wish to be let off the hook re my non-compete agreement," he laughed, "including the clause which allowed Saatchi to own my name for all time. I also confided that I'd be talking soon to venture capitalists about a possible LBO (Leveraged Buyout Offer)." Gideon had no qualms about sticking to his guns.

Meanwhile, Blackstone wrote a detailed descriptive document called, "the book" on Gartner that would be sent to potential purchasers. It contained the firm's financials, client lists, strategies, and much more. Gartner was officially for sale.

The Perils of Partnerships

Upon learning that "the book" on Gartner had been sent out to dozens of prospective suitors, Gideon immediately contacted Chris

Brody at E.M. Warburg Pincus and Neill Brownstein at Bessemer Ventures. They had been the original Gartner investors and a mainstay of the board from its founding to its sale to Saatchi. Chris and Neill both suggested that Gartner take a pre-emptive approach.

Throughout July 1989, as discussions with Chris progressed, Gideon recognized that management should be taking firmer control. This would mean that Gideon would need to make a huge commitment with regard to both his career and his financial investment. His company had been sold to Saatchi with a view of creating liquidity for Gartner's people and for himself, offering some freedom as a side benefit. Despite the success of Gartner, the firm had never been Gideon's entire life. His interests were diverse, and he had often longed for an opportunity to set out in new directions. Gideon had hoped the sale would result in what he called, "the light at the end of the tunnel."

At this critical juncture, Neill sat him down for a heart-to-heart. "Gideon," he said, "This is your opportunity to control your destiny. But you'll not be happy if you disengage completely from Gartner Group, so stay in control."

That piece of advice kept echoing in subsequent conversations with Chris. As their talks went on, it became increasingly clear to Gideon that Chris wished to take control of the company by owning two-thirds of the stock. Gideon started to develop major objections. Gideon remembered a particular meeting at Chris' office that ended in a proclamation. "Gideon," Chris said, as the men reached the doorway, "You need to look at the big picture. Remember, you have to be comfortable with your partners." The announcement backfired and made Gideon doubt whether he was comfortable enough with Chris' terms to want to be his partner, and he ultimately rejected Chris' offer.

But ultimately, the Chris Brody experience led to a positive conclusion for Gartner. Gideon resolved that Gartner would pursue the employee buy-back, and pull all strings to avoid working for someone else. He determined that outsiders — people with no prior stake in building this, the most influential company in the Information Technology world — were mainly interested in Gartner for the buck. But to Gartnerites their firm was a matter of life, and if they had any opportunity to control and benefit from its continued success, why shouldn't they pursue that goal?

Selling the company to any outsider would likely lead to a withering away of Gartner's carefully cultivated research and distribution arms; the two infrastructures upon which its entire business was based. If that were allowed to happen, Gartner would likely decline into a marginally profitable, undistinguished firm. Gideon couldn't allow that to happen. So he decided to make every employee a shareholder, as they had been in the earliest days of the firm. The first time Gartner Group was sold, five partners had each come out with over a million dollars and many other employees had earned capital gains in the hundreds of thousands. Gideon predicted that this time the returns could be much more substantial: he could create more millionaires, not to mention *scores* of half-millionaires!

To achieve this dream, Gideon knew he would have to aggressively pursue a management-led buyout of Gartner. This was an odyssey, but somehow, Gideon felt drawn to the necessity of this option. Gideon had learned a lesson from what had happened to some of the better players in the business when larger firms acquired them. The most blatantly obvious example was DataQuest. Gideon was very close to this firm while at Wall Street in the 1970s. It had been a vibrant and intellectually stimulating environment as it grew from its founding by David Norman and several partners to become a successful provider of market research information to computer and electronics information suppliers. DataQuest was sold in 1978 to AC Nielsen, which was in turn gobbled up by Dun & Bradstreet (D&B) in 1984. The founders soon left and D&B, despite periodic global announcements to the contrary, saw its baby falter, slow in growth momentum, and lose most of its market value. Had DataQuest remained under the leadership of its originators and personnel, Gideon thought, it might have survived.

His belief that Gartner should not be sold to an outsider was strengthened, but the fact remained – the company had been put on the market. If he were going to manage to achieve his lofty goals, he needed to start looking for an alternative solution, and quickly!

During the last two weeks of July, Gideon filled Gartner's calendars with meetings and phone calls involving a host of financial players presenting dozens of financing ideas and proposals; friends who were familiar with Gartnerite values were contacted and encouraged to dump any and all ideas into the Gartner database. Gideon's own notebook was a potpourri of spreadsheets and numbers crunched in a chaotic jumble. Meanwhile, he worried about being fired or sued – or both!

As the Chris Brody situation receded, Neill Brownstein stepped up to assert his own interest in buying the firm. Around the beginning of August 1989, Neill started to mention Dun & Bradstreet and Bain Capital with increasing frequently. Bain Capital was an investment company spun out from Bain Consulting, funded partly by Bain's partnership capital and partly by investors brought together by Bessemer Trust. Neill had learned that Bain was forming yet another spinout, later to be called "Information Partners" (IP). IP had obtained 51 percent of its capital from Bain, and the other 49 percent from D&B. Its purpose was to invest in information companies that were so small and risky that D&B could not or would not invest directly. Meanwhile, D&B created D&B Enterprises, which was set up to monitor this portfolio and to pursue other venture activities. Neill thought that Gartner would be an ideal early acquisition.

By mid-August of that year, Neill had organized a meeting at Bessemer's offices in Wellesley, Massachusetts. In attendance were Neill, Gideon, Grigs Markham (Gartner's CFO), D&B

Enterprises' president Dennis Cisco, and Steve Pagliuca (the senior man in IP). Neill suggested creating a deal structure that would be an LBO (Leveraged Buyout) including Bessemer and Bain as equity investors with D&B as a minority investor but with a significant share of the business accruing to Gartner employees. Gideon said it was an interesting idea, and the meeting broke up with no firm decision having been reached.

Gideon was convinced that any large corporate buyer would kill the firm. The benefit of having D&B as a minority investor was the potential for below-market rate debt financing coupled with an elimination of the largest potential corporate bidders for Gartner Group. The fact was, if D&B had already invested, no other corporation would likely be interested in making a bid for ownership. Additionally, D&B already owned Dataquest, and this suggested possible future operating synergies, an idea that delighted Gideon.

But then Gideon's paranoid streak emerged, and he wondered whether there might be a hidden agenda. The assumption was that D&B had been planning to bid, but through the grapevine (and Neill's involvement with Bain and IP), Gideon had learned that Dennis Cisco and the IP people were developing a parallel interest in going after Gartner. Thus, D&B might bid along one track and through its investment with IP, on the other track.

Gideon was suddenly struck by the notion that any bid by D&B was likely motivated by its problems as the owner of DataQuest, problems which had been inherited when it bought Nielsen several years earlier. It was possible that D&B wanted, not synergy, but a full merger. If Gartner Group were ever to be combined with DataQuest, the operational problems would be a nightmare. At the next possible opportunity, Gideon tried to convince Neill to write in language that would keep the two firms separate, but Neill wouldn't listen: he wanted to do a transaction, any transaction. Considering the Bessemer/IP joint history, Gideon suspected that Neill somehow owed Bessemer a transaction, and Garner would make them square.

Gideon addressed the issue by phone, voicing his fears. "Neill, it wouldn't work. I don't want to dilute our success, and I don't want to complicate our business more than it already is."

"Gideon, if you combined with DataQuest, you'd be by far the largest factor in the industry...you'd control it all."

"Yeah, Neill, but DataQuest needs what we do, while we don't need what it does. Ours is the hot growth market. They would just slow us down!"

"Don't jump to conclusions. You could probably spin off what you didn't want and you'd be able to select the executives from each company. You might even find among them your Chief Operating Officer."

Admittedly, Neill had his eye on all the important balls.

Gideon continued: "You know, Manny Fernandez (then CEO of DataQuest) may make an okay COO, but there's zero reason to think he could adapt to our vision or culture. Don't you know that DataQuest has worsened under him?"

"So you'll reform him or don't use him...look, D&B is a big company and has deep pockets. Its cash could make this deal happen."

"D&B had its chance," Gideon snapped. Before Saatchi had appeared on the scene, D&B had insulted Gartner in an open meeting by quoting a price that was so much below reality that Gideon had stalked out of the room in disgust. "Look, Neill, there's no reason to think that we could consolidate these companies efficiently, especially given the overlap and difference in culture. You've seen the scenario for 'Gartner Group in the Year 2000,' no? That's what is needed for us to succeed. It's our vision, and it calls for reinventing the company to create major growth, which won't happen without reinventing our approach. Nobody can come in and make that happen, we'll be tired and boring under an outside owner. *We* need to control Gartner!"

But on September 26, Dennis Cisco, Steve Pagliuca, and Bob White of Bain, visited Gartner Group to present their financing proposal. They made apologies for Neill, saying he was in London. Dennis began with the usual preliminaries, describing how Dunn & Bradstreet analyzed opportunity, trying to match it with strategic moves. He then evaluated Gartner's fit with the IP mission, considered the risks — it was all very standard, and Gideon sat back and took in the presentation while making his own judgment. The D&B point of view seemed to be that a deal with Gartner would unlock the door to a future combination with DataQuest, and the lack of a deal would create a destructive competition that would be of detriment to both firms. Gideon also sensed that despite the chatter, D&B was unlikely to make a high preemptive bid to buy Gartner.

Dennis continued, but the presentation veered to strange territory. D&B began to raise new concerns about issues Gideon thought they had long since reached agreement on: control of the board, the pension fund, value from "soft dollars" (sources of equity such as conversion moneys), and Gideon's own relatively high ownership percentage. This turn of the conversation made Gideon nervous. He tried to attribute Cisco's paranoia to the normal devil's advocate concerns that people who are to be principals in a deal feel free to express. Still, it was worrisome. If the firm was going to offer the top dollar that Gartner was worth, D&B should be more excited about their prospects.

As the meeting progressed into the wee hours of the morning, Gideon was finally handed the investor list. There was an obvious omission. Neill Brownstein's firm, Bessamer, wasn't listed. It had to be a mistake. Neill had been the one to invite Bain and D&B to participate in the deal in the first place!

Gideon asked, "What about Neill Brownstein and Bessemer?" After a brief silence, Cisco was the one to field a response: "The way we look at it, the deal is too small for both us and Brownstein."

Gideon was aghast. The meeting ended shortly thereafter, and he spent a sleepless night agonizing over this disappointing turn of events. He called his longtime supporter in London the next morning to tell him what had transpired. Neill listened quietly. When the whole meeting had been recapped, Neill proclaimed in a voice dripping with sarcasm: "Great guys."

The financial world is ultimately dog-eat-dog. In 1985, when Bain Capital was founded, Bessemer Ventures had introduced Bain to Bessemer Trust Company, which became the largest limited partner in Bain, accounting for about 25% of the assets Bain managed. Over the next four years, Bessemer had invited Bain into a number of deals, mostly in specialty retailing, including giants like Staples. Yet here was Bain, turning on Bessemer over Gartner.

D&B's Dennis Cisco soon put pressure on Gideon to consider and accept the Bain offer. He contended that he could only keep his company from making an offer to buy all of Gartner Group for two or at the most, three days. The clear implication, was that if Gartner refused the deal with Bain, then D&B would scoop up the firm. "In retrospect, I wish D&B had done so," Gideon recently admitted, "But we later discovered that D&B never had a real interest in buying us for its own account."

Gideon was not totally comfortable with Bain as an equity partner, and this affected the negotiations. However, after Bain grudgingly agreed to provide a token amount of equity for Bessemer, Gartner entered into a six-week period of negotiation on terms of their joint proposal to buy the company.

Gideon recalls the experience as terribly frustrating. "We were close to a deal, but D&B was off the mark with regard to understanding our true requirements," he recalled. "I suspected that the issues had to be reconcilable, but I was unable to make telling points in our conversations. As with many other negotiators, these people took a position, would not budge, and had a pat answer for any objection, or statement of need or want."

Time Out for Contemplation

Gideon found himself wondering what he had gotten into. He reached out to friends and business acquaintances for their opinions, perspectives and advice.

He first went to lunch with Charlie Ellis. Charlie was an ex-board member of Gartner and the managing partner of Greenwich Associates, an equally successful company in the financial services information business. Much more than just a consummate businessman, Charlie was also an historian, a teacher, writer, philosopher, and an outstanding speaker for his strongly felt ideas and ideals. Gideon bemoaned his lemming-like rush into the fray. Charlie had always supported Gideon's search for freedom from structure and corporate life, but this time, Charlie argued that Gideon should follow his instincts to fight for the buyback. Only Gideon could guess what would ultimately provide the greatest emotional returns.

Gideon also spoke at length with Michael Braude, Gartner's top analyst. Mike had been with the firm for years, and he and Gideon had become friends. Gideon respected his significant insight. Mike asked Gideon outright, "What do you really want to do?"

"I can't really figure that out," Gideon replied, "Except that it would be good to run our own show again, wouldn't it?" On the issue of creating great wealth for Gartner Group people, Mike said, "At this point you don't owe anything to anyone except yourself!"

Gideon later spoke to his son. Perry reminded him that he'd once told his son: If you are doing something for an obscure and unidentifiable reason then you ought to rethink.

Still, Gideon was confounded by the question. Why should he rush into a buyback that would straitjacket him for years into business activities he had just recently managed to finally eschew? He would again be responsible to others: all those who put their trust in him, the banks who assumed he would be committed to see this through, the equity investors (specifically Brownstein) and of course himself (especially if he put a significant amount of his own cash into the business). Jon Art, the talented corporate development staffer everyone called "Mr. Think-Tank" suggested

Gideon only put in that amount of capital which he would feel totally comfortable losing!

Then came the matter of succession. Gideon had been hoping to finally be able to address hiring someone to whom he could delegate complete authority as well as responsibility. But was a transition like this even possible? His mind said yes, but the track record of founders handing over the reins was historically dismal. Gideon decided to face this historical precedent and learn from it. It was likely that people in the Gartner business would continue to use him as a sounding board, even if this could interfere with the independence of a new chief executive, and so be it. The thing that actually made Gideon most nervous, was that if he saw the business turning sour, or starting to haphazardly change directions, he knew he was likely to feel compelled to raise questions — if not step right back into a leadership role!

The only way Gideon could see to guarantee his own freedom was to go with the Blackstone process, find the best buyer, and negotiate directly. This presumed that any private buyer would cut him a very rich deal. Ironically, while Gideon had the most to gain from a sellout to some large company with deep pockets, he also had the most to lose in an Employee Buyout (EBO), since he was planning an exceedingly broad stock distribution across the majority of the Gartner staff.

Gideon now entertained thoughts and dreams of ideas and intellectual pursuits he had neglected for decades. Having missed the annual humanitarian event called the Windstar Conference in Aspen, organized originally by John Denver and Buckminster Fuller, Gideon now held an invitation to the 1990 World Economic Forum in Switzerland, which he had attended two years prior. These were the types of activities that he hankered for: mind-expanding international events, sojourn teaching at the Aspen Institute, and other personally edifying experiences.

For example, his list of writing projects had expanded. Gideon had devised a regime whereby he'd pen or dictate a fixed number of pages per day to bring one or more of these projects to completion —but had not had the opportunity to put this plan into action. He had written to several deans at business schools and received a few replies expressing interest in further pursing the idea he might join their faculty. The ball was in his court. In addition, his daily practice of chess and piano had stagnated in the past few months, and perhaps serendipitously Gideon had bumped into a former piano teacher who encouraged him (as had other friends) to jump back in and expand his repertoire. There was a great deal that Gideon wanted to do – and all of it would require more free time than the CEO of a big company ever had.

Bert Fingerhut, an ex-partner at Oppenheimer, told Gideon that he should spend as much as a year analyzing his various options.

Yet Gideon felt inexorably pulled towards doing battle with Saatchi for ownership of what he still considered to be his company. Bombarded with signals and information pulling him in different directions, his inner voice told him that the real battle loomed: he was immersed in an important fight and he wanted to win!

IDC Plays Dirty Pool

In mid-September Gideon received an urgent internal call. "Did you see *Computerworld* this week?" *Computerworld* was the largest trade publication in the world. Gideon was urged to get hold of a copy ASAP and to find IDC's advertisement. The ad had been called to Gideon's attention on the Thursday after its publication on Monday. Gideon had a copy delivered and was staggered by what he saw.

Staring him in the face was an almost full-page photograph of Charles Greco, a vice president of International Data Corporation, the market research arm of International Data Group, which published *Computerworld*. The text of the ad was in two parts. The first was printed as though it was coming out of Greco's mouth, and it was signed by him. It said:

"THE GARTNER GROUP IS FOR SALE AGAIN. IT SEEMS NO ONE ELSE WANTS THEM, WHY WOULD YOU?"

The concluding text read:

Initially, Gideon didn't take the ad seriously. He laughed at the way that the speech bubble was signed, in a sort of overkill that was also grammatically weird. Was the guy saying his own name? The whole thing was so crass, it was sure to blow over, or at the very least, be seen as slanderous and reflect badly on the company that placed it. And after all, it was just one ad, probably a judgment error that escaped the checks and balances of the preeminent publication of the trade. *Computerworld* had an excellent reputation. They couldn't have agreed to this willingly. It had to be a mistake.

But his wheels started spinning. Gideon knew that Pat McGovern, the CEO and owner of International Data Group had been planning to make some sort of bid to buy Gartner at auction. Gideon assumed Pat, a longtime colleague, had not personally seen the ad before publication, but, of course, he couldn't be sure. Pat was reputedly a bottom bidder; could this be a strategy to drive the price down? Gideon couldn't believe that Pat would work in such a disgusting manner, and if that was the goal, Gideon was sure it would fail because the method was so transparent.

The following Monday, he bought *Computerworld* off a newsstand. Lo and behold, there was a follow-up ad:

197

There followed a short list of Gartner vice-presidents who had left
the business over a span of about one year, some voluntarily for
really big positions in industry, and a few who had been released
for various reasons. Charlie Greco's ad continued:

Gideon was flabbergasted. Had McGovern seen this? If so, he must
have approved it—but how could a colleague that Gideon knew
was a decent man have approved such outright slander? What was
going on? Gartner's management group huddled and decided to
take the strongest possible action. Gideon had alerted Blackstone
to the first ad but now called again and spoke at length with Austin
Beutner, an investment banker, who would have seen and discussed
it with Steve Schwartzman. Blackstone then would have contacted
Saatchi, because after all, IDC's parent IDG had indicated its
intent to enter the auction to acquire Gartner.

On September 20, Beutner wrote a memorandum to Pat
McGovern:

Dear Mr. McGovern:

We have been made aware of your recent advertising campaign.

We find such a campaign inconsistent with your letter to Andrew Woods of Saatchi & Saatchi, dated July 10, 1989, and inconsistent with any desire to acquire the Gartner Group. We also feel such actions are not in keeping with good faith business practices in our industry.

On behalf of Saatchi & Saatchi, we request (pursuant to Section 8 of the Confidentiality Agreement signed by International Data Group dated July 12th, 1989), that you promptly return to us all material that we furnished to you, and destroy all other related documents.

You are also reminded of International Data Group's obligations pursuant to the July 12 agreement.

Gideon then took the train to Manhattan to meet with Saatchi's lawyers. It had taken them a bit longer to respond than it took Blackstone, but their response was firm and must at least have caused some consternation in IDC's headquarters. A transmission was sent to IDC, *Computerworld,* and to its parent company, reading as follows:

We are the attorneys for Gartner Group, Inc. ("Gartner"). On September 11 and 18, 1989 advertisements were published in the periodical "Computerworld" on behalf of IDC Financial Services Corporation. Those advertisements falsely implied, among other things, that Gartner was financially unstable, "No one else wants them," and that specific key employees have left Gartner due to its alleged difficulties. We understand that IDG Communications controls both the source of these allegations and the media that disseminated them.

You must know or should have known that these statements are false. In our opinion your conduct is tortuous, otherwise unlawful, and subjects you to substantial liability to Gartner.

Gartner demands enforceable assurances that similar disparagements of Gartner will not be made in the future. In addition, appropriate reparative action including retraction of these statements must be made. In the absence of such assurances and reparative measures being taken, Gartner has instructed us to bring an action against each of you for injunctive relief, punitive damages and its attorneys' fees.

Gideon called *Computerworld's* editor-in-chief. He commiserated and admitted to his own shock over the second ad; the first ad had flown beneath the radar, but he now independently called IDC and unilaterally forbade continuation of the ugly ad campaign.

The IDC affair was temporarily closed. It would re-emerge when McGovern and his team visited Gartner a month later, in late October 1989. They had received Saatchi's "book" describing Gartner and wanted to acquire it.

Vive La France?

In early October 1989, Gideon had received an interesting phone call from Michel Jalabert at Capgemini Group. Jalabert was accelerating his own involvement by pursuing direct conversations.

He requested a private meeting to be informed of Gartner's needs and desires. Jalabert openly acknowledged that he was less interested in the actual percentage of his holding than in control. The huge French IT consulting company had offered Saatchi an outrageously large amount – well over $100 million, including some management equity participation – so at this point Saatchi was set to refuse Bain's bid for the company.

But while the Capgemini people were enamored of the idea of buying Gartner, they apparently didn't do enough homework. Gideon knew full well that a price of $100 million would not stick. They had hardly begun serious negotiations when the deal began to unravel.

Happy Anniversary

For Gartner's tenth anniversary on October 9th, 1989, Gideon threw an extravagant affair, its biggest party to date. In his public remarks Gideon told an old joke retrofitted to the circumstances: Mikhail Gorbachev, George Bush, and Pat McGovern are having a conversation with God. Gorbachev asks, "Dear God, is there any chance the US and Russia will ever make peace?" "Yes, Mikhail, but not in your lifetime." Bush then asks, "Holiest of Holies, is there any likelihood that the blacks and whites in our country will coexist in perpetual harmony?" "Yes, George," says God, "but not in your lifetime." Pat McGovern then speaks up. "Most Gracious Deity, is it possible that my company, International Data Group, and Gartner Group will ever be friends and partners?" God responds, "Yes, Pat, it is possible, but not in *my* lifetime."

Just two days later, on October 11th, Blackman's Schwartzman and Beutner were on a conference call with Gideon. Saatchi had decided to let IDG bid for Gartner despite its disparaging advertisements. Gideon went ballistic, exclaiming, "Saatchi is shooting itself in the foot again. I thought we were *suing* IDG. How can we let them bid? Everybody at Gartner would walk."

Schwartzman replied, "Look Gideon, we're boxed in. IDG's money is green and Saatchi wants to get the best price."

Gideon asked about the French deal.

The reply was that the French deal was not certain, but if it happened, so be it. This threw Gideon back into his rage. He pointed out that Saatchi just wanted to get the best price, even at the expense of the careers of everyone at Gartner. This was in direct conflict with its original representations that of having the interests of Gartner's people in mind and at heart. He went on to bluster to the effect that he hoped Saatchi *would* sell the company to IDG, just so that he could see the ensuing drama.

Steve asked, "How long do you think it would take to do your own deal?"

Gideon was silenced. When he recovered, he said, "If you come to the table with us now, only a few days."

He promptly brought his people together for an information exchange. Someone pointed out that both the *Wall Street Journal* and the *New York Times* had run articles just that morning rumoring that Saatchi & Saatchi was being taken over and was under pressure to rapidly sell its consulting companies.

On October 12th, Gideon took a meeting with the Dutch publishing house, Elsevier. They stayed over in Stamford, discovered that Gartner wanted to be allowed to function independently, and quickly passed, leaving the next day at noon.

And then, on October 16th, Gideon learned that the longtime CEO of Saatchi & Saatchi, Morris Saatchi, was being replaced by Robert Louis-Dreyfus.

IP is still in the Game

Even though Neill Brownstein had been dis-invited from the Dun & Bradstreet/Information Partners deal to acquire Gartner, he was not ready to retire from the action. He worked as best he could to put together a fresh deal which would be responsive to Gartner's needs, while maintaining conversations with D&B as a cooperative leader, possibly on the chance that he would be asked back in.

He pointed out that Gartner couldn't totally ignore its old "friends" IP (Information Partners), the fund under the Bain Capital umbrella, where 49% of the capital was Dun & Bradstreet money, and which had a mission to invest in information companies. Gartner's business would be a plum for IP's first investment, but its people continued to push for returns that were outrageous compared with anything that Gideon felt was appropriate for its money.

Gideon was becoming sick of people browbeating him that any deal was great. They might be getting tired of waiting, but Gideon was looking for the right deal, and he was sure it was out there somewhere. After all, Gartner Group *was* its people, and its people were all strong-minded individuals. If Saatchi sold the firm to a random company, it would not necessarily be able to deliver it intact!

However, the idea that others might accuse Gideon of obstructing their deals, kept him awake nights. He was working hard to help Saatchi sell the business at a decent price and Gartner had been a gracious host to all the possible bidders so far — except to IDG. Gartner explicitly played by the rules, and while Gideon wouldn't sign the Saatchi document that presented "Gartner for sale," he did succeed in adding a list of demands. Saatchi knew what elements would render a bill of sale unacceptable to Gideon.

IDG is Back in the Game

Despite their advertisements in *Computerworld*, rumors were spreading about a successful bid for the company by IDC, IDG's subsidiary. A fax arrived from Blackstone with a list of attendees for due diligence sessions on October 25th and October 26th. The list included Pat McGovern and a team of senior people from

IDG. In other words, IDG was definitely in the bidding to acquire Gartner from Saatchi.

Gideon and McGovern's friendship went back a long way, from MIT to IBM and the early days of IDC. But Gideon was angry because McGovern owned and controlled the media that had supported – or at least condoned – the advertisements that IDC was using to artificially lower Gartner's price. And now McGovern had come for a visit at Gartner?

Gideon entered the room, wearing a scowl. He sat down before the panel of six IDC people without saying a word. An eternity of seconds passed with no one speaking. McGovern broke the silence with an apology, and an attempt to gloss over what happened.

"I'm afraid I cannot accept your apology," Gideon replied. "Pat, the time to apologize was a month ago."

"Sorry, you're quite right, but I was out of the country."

Pat did travel constantly.

"Didn't anyone from IDC in a position of authority see your first ad in time to pull the second?" Gideon demanded.

"No," replied McGovern.

"Isn't the perpetrator of the ad an *officer* of your company?"

Everyone knew that the perpetrator was the President of IDC Financial Services Corporation, Charles Greco; after all, he had *signed* the ads.

McGovern replied, "He's the president of one of the IDC companies."

"Is he still there?"

"Yes, he's still there. I told him not to repeat the incident."

At Gartner, any individual who showed that level of misjudgment would be out of the company in a week, but McGovern appeared to be totally indifferent to the situation.

"The people who put the ad in didn't know that we were bidding for the company," McGovern added. Gideon bit back a retort that knowledge of an IDG bid would never have stopped Charlie from putting in the ads. His instinct told him that Charles Greco knew *precisely* what he was doing in lowering the IDG bidding price by frightening away other prospective buyers. Gideon knew that if he made this accusation, the meeting would become a free-for-all. He kept his opinions to himself and his comments civilized and short.

After the IDC presentation, McGovern called Gideon aside.

"How can we make this happen?" his longtime colleague asked, as if they were about to go for a round of golf. Gideon could not believe that his old friend was so totally oblivious to the message Gartner had been promulgating all morning.

Gideon replied, "Decide if you want to bid, and then deal with Blackstone. I can't get involved."

"How many bidders are there?" McGovern was treating Gideon as if nothing bad had ever passed between their respective companies. He chuckled. He put on the old-boy charm.

Gideon could not let go of his rage. "Ask Blackstone."

"Can't you give me some indication? If there are other bidders, we'll also feel forced to bid for your company."

"Perhaps Blackstone will tell you."

"Can't you give me *some* idea who else might be bidding?"

McGovern didn't let up. Gideon finally told him Gartner was putting together its own bid, but other than that, he politely refused to answer, playing it more straight with his colleague than even Blackstone could have hoped.

McGovern then offered to work with Gartner to help buy the company back. This startled Gideon. He responded that in putting together its LBO, Gartner was in fact considering a financial transaction and/or a strategic investment by a corporate firm. McGovern asked if IDC could discuss being that corporate partner. There followed a lengthy discussion.

For his part, Gideon made clear that help from McGovern would only be possible after it was firmly established that IDC would not be bidding independently. Blackstone viewed him as being an outside bidder, not involved with management, and anything Gideon could say to draw McGovern into direct discussions with management would therefore be inappropriate; Gideon's hands were tied. He could not discuss this topic further until IDC completed its due diligence and decided independently whether to bid for the company or not.

McGovern wouldn't give up. He asked what the chances were that Gartner might deal with him directly, if IDC did not bid.

"Pat," Gideon replied, "That would come down to a group of us sitting around a table, looking at what you had to offer versus what other people had to offer. I have to tell you, and you should understand based on this morning's proceedings, that the chances of our voluntarily wanting to work with you are very slim."

McGovern laughed.

It was clear now that IDG had never expected to pay Saatchi's full price, let alone put together a healthy incentive plan, invest further in putting solid management in place, or deal with Gartner's budget issues (for example, the expenses deriving from escalating attrition rates). Gideon had known McGovern for many years – the tactics were obvious. The man was wickedly intelligent, but ultimately not very nice. For him, it all came down to the bottom line.

Gideon was depressed by the whole process. McGovern showed insensitivity by acting as though he didn't care whether Gartner wanted to work with him or not. He also seemed not to care whether he bought the company against Gartner's will or on its behalf. And Gartner was still very much Gideon's baby. He cared a great deal that the business be a place that people enjoyed working; that the work be personally edifying to himself and all other Gartnerites. During this meeting, Gideon realized that above all, he had hoped that the people who worked at Gartner would think of each other as a *family*. Would think of their work as *fun*. Gideon decided that dealing with IDC would be no fun at all. They were a classless bunch of money-grubbing businessmen with no sense of loyalty, and Gideon felt that working with them in any way would mark the end of Gartner Group as a quality institution.

The French Deal

Then, on the morning of November 7, Austin Beutner of Blackstone called Gideon, asking if he was prepared to hear the terms which Blackstone had negotiated with the French. Beutner sounded smug. The deal was $100 million cash, except that Saatchi would retain responsibility for the incentive stock options and Fund A payments which had a present value of about $7 million. A couple of other adjustments, and the effective price dropped to about $90 million.

Twenty million more than we had been prepared to offer. Gideon was frustrated. He had hoped that Gartner's LBO alternative could come to terms with the French for $70 million, a reasonable price, which (while not providing top dollar to Saatchi) was still above what Gartner could produce on an LBO basis.

It was a truly credible value for the Gartner asset.

But this new offer put the affair in jeopardy. The situation that presented itself now seemed to be pretty clear: A realistic price level of $80 million cash would be feasible for all parties and likely result in a fair price to Saatchi at a higher level than what it might ultimately receive.

But again, Gideon's instinct rankled. Something was wrong with the $90 million offer, but what? The answer hit him like a bombshell. The French had made no attempt to speak to Gartner's management. If the possible French deal was at all to be contingent on agreement with Gartner's management, and Capgemini had been ready to overpay by $10 to $20 million, before even *speaking* with the people at Gartner, how could such an economic deal be rationalized and why even enter into serious discussion with them? Would the French be half as generous with the people at Gartner who would make the company successful, as they were planning to be with Saatchi? They should have insisted to Saatchi that they would *first* agree on a deal with management as its partner and *then* negotiate a price. This was the way to treat a real partner.

Gideon's instinct was to walk away.

But Jalabert called him at home to review the terms of the deal. They argued a bit as he tried to convince Gideon that Gartner would certainly have independence. Gideon considered his argument a sham, and assumed the deal would be viewed as a buyout, instead of Gartner obtaining independence in any real sense. For Gartner, independence had to include determining its own ultimate fate.

Jalabert swiftly rejoined: "Isn't IDG the alternative?"

Gideon told him that he did not take IDG seriously, and that none of his staff had any interest in working for IDG.

At which moment, it was likely that Jalabert realized that he had indicated too high a price to Saatchi.

It turned out, though, that things might turn out well for Gartner if it was bought by Capgemini. After this conversation with Jalabert, Gideon thought it was quite possible that the French might come to terms contractually and agree that their first priority would be succession. But the aspect of the French deal that Gideon felt could be real a swing factor was that they had also hinted about sweetening the contract. If this were true, then Gartner could have its cake and eat it too! Partners could soon lock in absolute returns of $100 million, triple what management would have received from an independent sale of the company.

On the other hand, few at Gartner liked Capgemini, possibly because too many of their people came off poorly. The French firm had average annual revenues-per-employee of well under $100,000 (at the then francs-per-dollar ratio) compared to Gartner's of over $200,000. The French company's culture was significantly different, and was expected to remain different. In discussions with Gartnerites, some thought that perhaps the Capgemini people "did not know what they did not know," and that "their view that they would be *helping* us might be a euphemism for *interfering* with us."

On November 14, Gideon received a letter from Saatchi's vice chair, advising Gartner that Saatchi & Saatchi had agreed in principal with Capgemini to sell it all of Gartner's capital stock. This letter hit Gideon like a sledgehammer. It effectively told him that this was the deal, and Gartner should discontinue any planning or negotiations relating to a management buyout of the firm.

Gideon immediately huddled his entire senior management team. In a pursuit of some "good faith" process, they composed a lengthy letter to Jalabert emphasizing Gartner's desire to insure a sound foundation for ongoing success, but reiterating that Gartner employees believe that the Gartner company functions best as an independent entity.

Within days, Jalabert wrote a letter to be distributed directly to all employees. Of course, this invited direct responses. These included such notes as: "My advice is that for your own benefit, in order to avoid wasting your resources you should forget about acquiring Gartner Group. It really won't work." Capgemini got the message loud and clear. Gartner's management was certain that the French deal was for all practical purposes, dead.

The Pressures of Passing Time

It had been six months since Saatchi had disclosed its intention to divest Gartner. Between the back-and-forth with Capgemini and Blackstone, Gideon felt valuable time slipping away. In the event that the French deal didn't happen, the company could not be much longer in limbo. If he waited until the French negotiations played out and then failed, Gartner would only then be starting due diligence discussions with IP, pushing closure further out into the future. Meanwhile, there was word that potential buyers for Hay Group (another Saatchi-owned consulting firm which was likewise on the block) had fallen by the wayside and Hay was ready to present its LBO to Blackstone. Gideon wanted Gartner's potential LBO to have an equal chance, especially if the French would not come around to Gartner-friendly views about independence and equity!

As the first two months of 1990 unfolded, the issue of bringing in an effective Chief Operating Officer (COO) became more pressing. Gideon was spread thin, overseeing far too many operational parts of the business while trying to arrange to buy the company back.

Then two news items appeared that spurred Gideon into action.

First, Michael Armellino, the partner in charge of research at Goldman Sachs, announced he was leaving the general partnership and becoming a limited partner. He would leave some capital in the firm and act as a consultant, but he would also have time to pursue his interests in history and political science, and also make time to teach and to travel. Overcome by jealousy, Gideon turned to the Arts section, hoping for a distraction.

There, Gideon read of the decision by Riccardo Muti to give up the directorship of the New York Philharmonic Orchestra and become "Laureate Conductor." His reasons: He wanted to spend more time with his family in Italy and less time conducting. Muti said, "It is now for me to have some time for myself instead of jumping from one part of the world to another, conducting and handling all the problems and responsibilities connected with being a music director. I need time to not only be a musician but a man of culture."

Gideon remembered his swirling thoughts: "I thought, 'If he can say it, so can I!' I was sure I could be 'Laureate CEO' or 'CEO Emeritus,' leaving me in some leadership position while allowing much delegation to a new executive. I jumped on the project of locating a COO with renewed vigor!"

There was no one in Gartner qualified for the task, so Gideon made up his mind to find the best possible candidate from the outside. He developed a short list of eight names and seriously pursued several, but one after another fell out of the running. One candidate asked for a $1 million sign-up bonus. Another, although clearly creative and outstanding, upon further checks, didn't seem likely to fit into the Gartner culture.

Finally, Gideon met with Manny Fernandez, who was earning a base of $210k and a bonus target of $150k as the CEO of DataQuest, one of Gartner's larger competitors. He'd been CEO of three companies and before that, the youngest VP at Fairchild Camera; he was also said to be truth-oriented, loyal, and knew how to deal with people. In initial conversations, he seemed to have no ego problem with being COO, i.e. under Gideon on the ladder, but in discussions of his objectives, said he wished to be "his own man." Gideon liked him.

Saatchi Shifts Course

Soon after Robert Louis-Dreyfus became the new CEO of Saatchi, he visited Gartner Group. There he told Gideon and a group of vice presidents that he did not believe the company could be sold to anyone other than its employees, but that he wanted to structure a deal in which Saatchi would maintain a significant minority ownership stake in the company. Quite a turn-about, and one that excited Gideon and his team. They immediately brought a broad proposal to Saatchi. But Dreyfus did not respond either then or to later requests for an answer. By early January, 1990, Saatchi informed Gartner it was keeping the firm on ice and was in no rush to dispose of it.

However, at the end of January, Dreyfus revisited Gartner's Stamford, CT offices for a two-day business review. At Gartner's request, he had agreed to reopen the firm's attempt to buy the company. With most of the details determined by Dreyfus himself, the outlines of a deal were quickly sketched whereby the employees of Gartner Group would buy 55% of the company in return for a $32 million payment (already lined up from other sources) to Saatchi. Before leaving, Dreyfus reiterated that a deal in which Saatchi was a significant minority investor was the only deal it would consider, and there would be no room for outside equity investors in such a deal.

Eight days later, on February 8, Gartner executives held a negotiating meeting with Saatchi at the offices of Dreyfus' family firm in New York. At the end of this meeting, they had nominally concluded the terms of a deal. The "would-be agreement" now called for the participation of the Gartner Group pension plan as an investor, so that every employee of the company could participate in the ownership of the Gartner business. Many of the specific terms, such as those relating to Saatchi's ability to later sell stock back to Gartner Group, were developed in detail by Dreyfus.

But then, just as progress was certain, things stalled. Saatchi stopped responding to communications, and started throwing up objections to points agreed upon at the February meeting. Gartner contacted its attorneys, who believed that the objections — all couched as legal issues — were strictly red herrings designed to stall the deal!

This put Gideon over the edge. Once again, he quietly reached out to select equity investors to see if it would be possible to construct a deal whereby Gartner employees bought 100% of the company from Saatchi. Among the investor groups contacted was again Bain Capital.

Back in November, Bain had faxed over an attractive term sheet. It provided Gartner employees with 58% ownership of the company plus the issuance of 1.7% incremental ownership each year for five years through the issuance of stock options. It had seemed promising.

On May 18, Gideon met with Dreyfus to negotiate a final term sheet. A full staff of lawyers from each side were also in attendance. Expectations were that negotiations would last through the night. Much to Gideon's chagrin, Dreyfus admitted he had not reviewed the proposal faxed to him by Gartner attorneys three days earlier and was therefore not ready to negotiate at the session. Though this was no different from the way Gartner had been treated throughout months of negotiations, Gideon's patience was wearing thin. The next week, Saatchi responded to Gartner's term sheet with several specific criticisms, but contributed nothing else to move the ball forward.

On the morning of May 24, Gideon was at the San Francisco airport with his two daughters, Sabrina and Aleba, waiting to board a plane for a Hawaii vacation. From a last minute phone conversation, he learned that Dreyfus was planning to fly that same evening from New York to Helsinki. Gideon devised a plan. He contacted Dreyfus' London office, found out his seat number, and, as luck would have it, was able to reserve a seat right next to his first-class, first-row seat! He told his daughters that unfortunately he would not be going with them to Hawaii but that they should continue as planned; he was sure they would have a great time. Gideon grabbed a flight back to JFK and rushed to board the plane to Helsinki!

Of course, Dreyfus was shocked when Gideon sat down next to him. Gideon informed him about San Francisco and his daughters and their aborted plans, but said that this seemed to be the only way they could move negotiations forward! Gideon didn't know what he had been expecting, but it wasn't this: Dreyfus dropped a bombshell. Saatchi, he said, had just granted an exclusive right to buy Gartner Group to an unnamed third party, and furthermore, during the "exclusive" period, Gartner was forbidden from pursuing its employee buyout. Dreyfus said that Gartner would be informed of Saatchi's intentions on June 15, and that was the end of the conversation. He turned away and napped the rest of the transatlantic flight. Gideon didn't get any sleep. He spent the night kicking himself for not going to Hawaii with his daughters.

Information Superhighway

Gideon soon unearthed the name of the third party. One of Gartner's senior employees had initiated a friendly call to Steve Pagliuca of Bain Capital and had somehow divulged the exact

Saatchi status including price information. Pagliuca immediately placed a call to Dreyfus and obtained the inside track to an advantageous and exclusive negotiation period. Gideon was swift to notice that Dreyfus had recently represented to Gartner that Saatchi would not negotiate with anyone but management, and equally vexing, Saatchi had never offered Gartner the opportunity to bid for 100% of the company before it entered into this exclusive with Bain.

Despite his relief that the mysterious "third party" was a familiar player, Gideon felt it prudent to continue searching for a deal to buy the entire company, in case the Bain situation did not develop. Heller Financial revealed it would be interested in providing approximately $40 million in debt. Gartner thought it could raise $4 million from employees and another $4 million from its pension plan. Neill Brownstein also said that Bessemer was interested in investing $4 million to $8 million in the company. To indicate Gartner's serious intention to buy the company; their investment bankers, Shearson, sent Saatchi a proposal on June 27 representing a new offer to buy the entire company for $61 million in cash and notes, emphasizing that Gartner was willing to negotiate all aspects of the deal including price.

Saatchi never responded to the letter.

Instead, Dreyfus called Gideon on July 2nd and informed him that a deal to sell the company had been struck. Gideon was then in

Edinburgh and agreed to meet with Dreyfus and Pagliuca in London on July 4th.

At the meeting, Gideon expressed shock that Bain had abused its privileged position as Gartner's LBO partner. Gideon remembered the meeting: "I told them that while I supported Saatchi's legal right to do anything it wished, Bain should share the company's equity with our employees as we had discussed in our negotiations in the fall. I reminded them that this approach would provide the same money to Saatchi and the same percentage return on investment to Bain. However, it would also create sufficient equity to motivate a large number of Gartner employees in what would be a very tight operating environment with a large amount of debt." Pagliuca responded that low interest rates early in the deal would not cause normal LBO strains, and that this was a good deal for the people. Bain claimed it, too, was a white knight because both IDG and another bidder, Ziff-Davis, had made brand-new offers to buy Gartner Group and were waiting to jump in if anything negative happened to Bain's deal.

Gideon was flying blind. The whole thing might have been a complete smokescreen but what he knew was that Gartner would never work with IDG and everyone knew too little about Ziff-Davis. With regard to the firm's staying as independent as possible, the Bain deal was the best offer yet.

The Outcome

The next day, Gideon wrote an all-company memo announcing the deal. He indicated that it was subject to thirty days of due diligence and that significant equity in the company would be set aside for management and other employees, but that details were not yet available. Bain must have known that to satisfy Gartner's team, the deal would have to mirror earlier discussions. Thus, a deal was negotiated resulting in sufficient equity to make most Gartner employees wealthy when Gartner went public again in 1993. It was a great coup for every Gartnerite.

Those of who fought for independence won. Gartner essentially converted what it hoped would be a management buy-out (MBO) to a tolerable leveraged buy-out (LBO). Gideon recently remarked, "I am convinced that Gartner would not exist at all today had my team not succeeded in acquiring the firm from Saatchi."

From an entrepreneurial perspective, here are the financial returns:

In 1979, when Gartner was initially funded to the tune of $50,000 in cash, besides a significant compensation reduction compared with his Oppenheimer earnings, Gideon's own investment for one-third of the equity in this new company was only one-third of $50,000, or $17,000. The VCs put in an additional $625,000 as redeemable preferred stock. After two later splits, the cost base to employees was two cents per share, 25% of which was subsequently sold for $10.50 a share when Gartner went public in 1986, and 75% at $22.50 a share when Saatchi bought the firm.

The Saatchi deal resulted in 40% of the new Gartner firm flowing to Gartner employees after they repurchased their company in 1991. By 1993, when the firm was taken public again, the *New York Times* reported that over 150 of Gartner's employees immediately became millionaires. Gideon was proud.

Manny Fernandez, whom Gideon had so liked, ultimately was hired by Gartner as its COO, with an agreement by Gideon and Gartner's Board of Directors that he would eventually be promoted to CEO. Gideon would happily become Chairman fourteen months later in April 1991.

Chapter 13: Making It Happen... Again.

Of course, Peter Wright was right when he predicted, "Gideon will keep starting new businesses until the day he's in his coffin, and maybe even after."

Even during Gartner Group's glory days in the late 1980s, Gideon had been noodling with the idea of a new and improved version of the company. "I already had in mind a better solution from the customer's perspective," he recalls. "If Gartner could implement it, then theoretically someone else could, too."

Of course, as long as he was running Gartner, he had neither the time nor the inclination to launch another company. But by 1991, Gideon was no longer running Gartner. Tired and bored, he had voluntarily quit being CEO, remaining as Chairman. But then Gartner's new CEO, Manny Fernandez, wished to be both CEO and chairman, and with backing from his board, Gideon separated from his namesake firm. Perhaps because Gideon knew the IT industry from top to bottom, the idea of a better Gartner popped up again in his mind – "and when I have a new idea, I like to try to implement it."

The more he considered, the more enamored he was by the possibilities of what a new company could do in the marketplace – and opportunities happened to be open to him. He explained, "Nobody thought I would start another company competing against Gartner Group, so I hadn't been asked to sign a Gartner Group non-compete clause. I was a free bird. I started to think about a new company design. Whenever I start anything new, I take a clean sheet of paper and start drawing pictures. Then I erase and go through iteration after iteration. I try to define what a new IT company might ideally look like. That's how Giga was born."

With the record of his stunning success at Gartner Group, raising money wasn't a problem. Gideon approached Neill Brownstein and some of the other original Gartner Group investors, as well as other acquaintances with money to invest, and found that he could come up with a "friends and family" round to help kickstart the development of a new company.

"I also put a couple of million bucks of my own into it, a lot more money than I would put in today to this sort of company," he noted, adding, "I don't know what drove me to invest that much money." By comparison, the $17,000 Gideon had put into the fledgling Gartner Group seemed like peanuts, even allowing for inflation. By December 1995, he had raised more than $15 million. Giga Information Group – the name was both a nod to the increasingly trendy use of computer terminology in everyday speech and a neat mash-up of the first two syllables of Gideon Gartner – was on its way.

Word of this new venture was soon out and the technology consulting industry was buzzing. A *BusinessWeek* article[9] asked the question on everyone's mind: "Can Gideon Gartner do it again?" The article noted, "Gideon Gartner's risks have paid off before." But it also warned of the challenge: "Giga Information Group plans to sell expert analysis of information-technology trends and products. It's a hot field these days, but the move puts Gartner on a collision course with the firm he co-founded in 1979: Gartner Group Inc., the business' $229 million-a-year leader."

Gideon noted, "Of course, I didn't think that Gartner could be unseated but I thought it could be penetrated to some small extent.

Why another startup at age 62, the article asked, when he could be practicing classical piano in one of his homes in Aspen or St. Thomas or Westport or New York?

Publicly, Gideon took an amused stance: "I just massaged this idea. I don't know if it was ego-fulfillment, to show if I could do it again." But to his closest friends, he revealed his true impetus: The prospect of competing against a company that already bore his name was a thrill.

"It kept my blood flowing. It was fun. The idea was a little bit far out but it was an adventure," he recalled.

---

9 "Gideon Gartner's New Trumpet." BusinessWeek, December 3, 1995.
http://www.businessweek.com/stories/1995-12-03/gideon-gartners-new-trumpet

Competition for a new company – even one with the brand value of the Gartner name – would be fierce. Thanks to the success of the first company Gideon had started and the growth of the field he had created and nurtured, there were now many info-tech advisory firms in operation: Gartner Group, Inc., Forrester Research, Jupiter Research, and META Group, which itself had been started by Gartner alumni – to name just a few. Market research firms, the "Big Six" accounting firms, consulting companies and systems integrators had also jumped into this lucrative space. An increasing number of companies which once would have been prime customers were now using their own internal planning, research and marketing staffs to dig up information – a kind of "Do-It-Yourself" data-mining. As noted in the description of Giga filed with the U.S. Securities and Exchange Commission, "Some of the Company's direct and indirect competitors also have established research organizations with greater market recognition and experience in the IT industry."

The filing further warned, "While [Giga] believes it can compete successfully on the basis of price, quality, distinctiveness, and responsiveness to customers, there are [a] few barriers to entry into the Company's market and new competitors could readily seek to compete in one or more market segments addressed by the Company's services. There can [also] be no assurance that the Company's current or potential competitors will not develop services comparable or superior to those developed by the Company or respond more quickly to new or emerging industry trends or changing customer requirements. There can be no assurance that the Company will be able to compete successfully against existing or new competitors."

However, as the SEC filing also pointed out, there was plenty of demand.

Gideon believed the IT information service industry was outmoded, stuck in what he called "the second generation model" prevalent in the 1980s. That model – pioneered by Gideon's Gartner Group – typically provided multiple information service offerings, each of which focused on a specific subject within the IT industry. For example, Gideon wrote in the SEC filing, "A second-generation provider might offer separate service offerings addressing mainframes, personal computers, operating systems, application development tools and relational databases."

However, times had changed.

Gideon wrote: "Historically, IT users would typically purchase a vertically integrated solution involving hardware, operating systems and application software from a single large vendor. In the current environment, IT users must evaluate a variety of products based on emerging technologies from multiple vendors and design systems in which the products operate with one another, with existing legacy systems and, increasingly, within the internet and emerging corporate intranet environments."

Users were confronted not only with an increasing number of technological choices but also with a proliferation of advice and information from multiple independent sources, such as newsletters, trade publications, the World Wide Web, the news media, and vendors. "This glut of information," the SEC filing went on, "makes it difficult for users to find the particular analysis and expertise that is most relevant to their particular operational needs and can lead to information-anxiety, confusion and frustration."

In short, even as organizations were making substantial financial commitments to IT systems and services, IT products were becoming increasingly complex and diverse, and the rate of technological change and new product introductions was accelerating. Even though many organizations maintained an internal staff of IT professionals and also engaged outside consultants to assist in IT "decision support," these same organizations often required greater capabilities than they could feasibly support internally and a more integrated approach than individual consultants could provide.

As a result, they increasingly turned for assistance to providers of Continuous Information Services (CIS) which continuously monitor and analyze IT industry developments and trends and provide reports and information to clients on a subscription basis.

But thankfully for Gideon, those CIS providers were themselves mired in a second-generation business model that did not provide integrated or cost-effective support for the customer or fulfill the evolving needs of IT users, vendors and investors.

"Customers were facing issues that transcended these sectors," Gideon said in an interview, "and were being asked to buy more and more services all the time. But the old model simply wasn't appropriate for the user constituency anymore."[10]

The Giga Solution

Giga, Gideon proclaimed in a *BusinessWeek* article, would run on an "entirely new business model." To begin with, instead of the multiple-service offerings that were a hallmark of Gartner Group (and several other firms, which had imitated Gartner's success), Giga would create an integrated single-service approach to address customers' needs. At a time when the Internet was first being compared to a fire hose spewing information out at customers without a way to separate useful data from junk, an integrated compact data delivery format would be different and greatly appreciated.

As with Gartner Group, Giga's customers would include: users and vendors of IT hardware, software and services, and institutional investors. Detailing the potential customer needs further, Gideon

---

10 "The Patriarch: Gideon Gartner, Giga Information Group." Information Week, November 17, 1997.

explained that decision-making by users had become increasingly complicated as the pace of technological change continued to accelerate. As a result, IT users required current information and analysis of new product introductions and other events, independent comparisons among competing platforms and vendors, accurate assessments of trends such as pricing and obsolescence, and reasoned analysis of how issues will evolve over time. Gideon believed that users would seek alternative points of view and rely on the advice and insights of more than one CIS provider. He noted that vendors used CIS primarily for product planning, evaluation of their competitors' products and for formulation of marketing and other business strategies. Vendors also required a reliable source of information on areas such as new markets and market forecasts, competitive products, user preferences and buying trends, distribution and marketing strategies, and evolving market needs. Meanwhile, institutional investors required CIS to evaluate user and vendor strategies, new IT product performance, product purchase expectations, and evolving market trends. By gaining timely access to appropriate information and using it in their company and industry analyses, institutional investors would be able to make more informed decisions and enhance their ability to make successful IT investments. Gideon proposed to meet each and every one of these needs with Giga. According to the SEC filing, the bywords guiding Giga were "comprehensive and customized Continuous Information Services."

Giga's Methods

First and foremost of the offerings was the Giga Advisory Service, providing information and advice from analysts by phone, conferences, electronic forums and teleconferences, in an integrated, single-service offering for an annual subscription fee.

Knowing that customers generally wished to consider a range of opinions and perspectives, Giga also offered access to its ExpertNet network of external IT practitioners, as well as a planned series of specialized research products, called Relevance Services, which combined original analysis, data and information produced by proprietary surveys and methodologies with consulting, to assist in enhancing the IT practices and operations of Giga's customers.

To make sorting through the full spectrum of Giga's original research and third-party content easy and efficient, the company leveraged the latest technological innovations to design GigaWeb, an Internet-based interface to its services and products. Using intelligent software search agents called Gigabots, customers could smoothly navigate through the full spectrum of the company's available information and, based on the customer's profile, search for and obtain information most relevant to their particular needs.

GigaWeb was just one differentiator, Gideon recalled. "At the time, everybody else was just porting their published information to the web. GigaWeb was interactive. Relatively speaking, it was plain vanilla but it was an advance compared with our competition. I don't think people ever did business with us because of GigaWeb, but in the context of our functional ideas that were attractive, it helped."

Another differentiator was born when Gideon recognized that people were overwhelmed by too much information. Gideon's solution was the Gigabyte. The Gartner Group "green sheet" had been an industry innovation, condensing many pages of overly complicated detail onto two sides of a single page. The Gigabyte further distilled data into its absolute essence: a quarter- to a half-page nugget of necessary information.

Gideon now says, "Were I to design a new Advisory, I would likely reduce the average length still further!"

Gaining Momentum

Gideon knew he worked best in tandem with a trusted subordinate. He said, "I don't think I would have started Gartner Group if I hadn't found David Stein." During the post-Gartner, early-Giga period, Neill Brownstein introduced him to David Gilmour, who had held various senior executive positions at Lotus Development Corporation (its "Lotus 1-2-3" spreadsheet was the first killer app for personal computers). Gideon recalled, "I was completely taken by his intelligence and his knowledge. He was living in California but I persuaded him to temporarily move East and work with me to develop Giga. Then he soon became the number two guy." Other members of the start-up team included two Gartner alumni, one to help develop the technology plan and another who provided marketing expertise.

With the team in place, Gideon started transforming his idea into reality.

Gideon's reputation helped boost Giga's initial momentum. However, to provide industrywide coverage in a single service, Giga had to hire expertise in all areas at once, rather than build up slowly. To achieve the kind of growth that would be required to establish a significant presence in its industry, Giga had to hit the ground at a full-out sprint.

"It's a difficult model to implement," Gideon later admitted to *Information Week*. "The cost structure coming out of the box was exceedingly high. That's implicit in the model we chose. We had to provide coverage over the entire industry before we signed up a single customer. We need[ed] to ramp up very quickly to reach a break-even point."[11]

Gideon's solution: "We should acquire a company that would provide a kind of base, and perhaps solve some of the early implementation challenges every start-up has," he recalled. "Their infrastructure would hasten our ability to enter the market and would also give us a revenue base."

---

11 Ibid.

As luck would have it, as Giga was being launched, Gideon was visited by Norman Pearlstein, president of Friday Holdings, which had acquired BIS Strategic Decisions from NYNEX and was now looking to sell it. (Pearlstein had also been the executive editor of The *Wall Street Journal*.) "It was a market research firm in technology, but it ventured beyond the scope of, let's say, Gartner Group's technology operations," Gideon said. "It got into printers, other hardware, and various niches of the marketplace. It had a good reputation and was about a $27 million company."

Gideon asked a former administrative assistant at Gartner Group who had become a venture capitalist to help with the acquisition. "With his negotiation skills, we acquired this $27 million company for next to nothing — $2 million!" Gideon said.

Unfortunately, this was one of those instances where a big discount came at a huge cost. Gideon noted, "Even though we did due diligence before buying BIS, there were so many skeletons in the closet! We paid only $2 million but inherited a sizable number of senior analysts and salespeople. BIS customer satisfaction had been declining and our model differed greatly. We decided to keep BIS's beautiful headquarters in the outskirts of Boston, its salesforce and several selected analysts, all of whom seemed happy to switch to the new business, and close down virtually every revenue center of that firm at great expense. We were private at that time, so the cost didn't really matter, but the management time that we absorbed was unreal. However, it gave us the infrastructure that we were looking for." Gideon concluded, "While we did spin out almost all the BIS revenue, the acquisition did enable us to get a quick start."

It was *déjà-vu* all over again – only with the accelerator jammed to the floor. With its fresh model and Gideon's reputation, Giga had contracts with more than 100 customers within its first year. By targeting large customers, Giga could boast such blue-chip names as AIG, Boeing, Hewlett Packard, IBM, KPMG, Oracle, and Southwestern Bell Telephone. Under Gideon's leadership as chairman and CEO, he recalled, "We were on a hot streak, growing much faster than Gartner ever grew. We booked our first revenues on April 1st, 1995, and by 1999 Giga's run rate exceeded $65 million."

Giga's growth can best be understood by looking at each year's "Annualized Value of Contracts," known simply as AV:

- 1996: $9,339,000 (N.B.: Giga only began selling on April 1)
- 1997: $26,619,000
- 1998: $43,799,000
- 1999: $58,061,000
- 2000: $63,169,000

At the same time, Giga continued expanding its breadth of research, employing fifty in-house analysts and establishing relationships with over two hundred external IT practitioners as part of its ExpertNet network. It was expanding its relationships with existing customers through its Relevance Services, as well as events, publications, consulting and econometric forecasting. It conducted operations in England, France, Germany, Italy, Korea and Australia, with plans to expand further. It planned to double its domestic sales force over the next six months, expand its domestic marketing organization, and create a domestic telemarketing group.

Through its acquisition of BIS, Giga acquired a conference development and management operation, and was soon producing day-long events and shorter briefings every month. Strategic alliances with prominent industry associations, consulting firms, and publishing houses enhanced the quality of its conferences and helped build awareness of the Giga name.

In addition, Giga offered online discussion groups for customers with shared interests to interact in an electronic forum, and GigaTels, audio teleconferences hosted by analysts and providing an open forum for questions and debates.

Striving for Break-Even

But from the very beginning, frustrations hobbled the exciting possibilities. The Giga model required rapid sales growth because, as Gideon noted, "Giga was going to deal with large enterprises, so we had to be able to respond to 95 percent of all of the issues which IT organizations were experiencing." Gartner had started with one service and then added other services incrementally; everyone knew that what they were getting was a piece of the entire spectrum of IT. At Giga, Gideon explained, "We were going to be all things to all people." Consequently, he said, "From Day One we had to be there with enough analysts. We hired over thirty analysts before we actually started to sell aggressively because we felt that with fewer than thirty people we couldn't compete against the Gartner Group."

Gideon put together a chart denoting Giga's knowledge base of analysts compared to the total number of dimensions in the very complex IT world. "If we covered enough, we were ready to go," he recalled. "But it was costing us money to put this analyst team together before there was any revenue whatsoever, so there were very high fixed costs."

If you draw a diagram showing the high fixed costs and revenue growth beginning from zero, assuming that your revenue grows in a straight line, at some point the two will intersect. That's the break-even point. If you grow too slowly, your break-even point will be way out in the future. The result: "You're going to run out of cash," Gideon said. That was the omnipresent threat to Giga: Not *would it succeed,*' but '*could it succeed fast enough?*'

That urgency also drove hiring of the sales force. "Once we had the analyst team, we said, 'Okay, now we're going to deliver our first product.' This was April 1, 1996," Gideon recalled. "We felt we had to have enough sales people in place to grow rapidly. We had to increase the analytic organization and the sales organization. There was no choice."

Always, always, there was the industry drumbeat urging Giga on against its chief competitor: Gartner Group. Gideon knew what potential customers would think as they considered switching from Gartner Group to Giga – and how Gartner Group would react. "Because of the single-service approach, somebody could get access to a broad spectrum of knowledge for a lot less money with Giga than with Gartner Group," Gideon said. "Gartner had to have layer upon layer of services to have equal coverage. So we knew that Gartner would respond to us by cutting prices. If we grew slowly, if we didn't have complete coverage in the United States, then every time Gartner was in a difficult competitive situation, they would drop their price to meet our price or do whatever they had to do to keep the business. I knew the way they thought. I would have done the same thing.

"If you're competing across the board, then they've got to cut their prices across the board," he continued. "However, they wouldn't be able to afford to keep doing that because they were a public company. At the very least, in their short-term financial performance, this approach would affect their profit and loss dramatically. That was another strategic reason why we had to grow rapidly." The strategy also added an extra element of risk: Could Giga blast past Gartner Group or were Gartner Group's resources deep enough to withstand repeated price cuts?

Further complicating matters was the fact that Giga was a virtual company. Unlike Gartner Group, where for the first several years, all of the sales people were in one room and all of the analysts in another and everyone was crammed under the same roof, Giga was literally spread all over the country. The company was headquartered in Boston, because BIS Strategic Decisions' main campus was located there, and Giga had kept most of its beautiful buildings and equipment. David Gilmour, Giga's number two guy, continued to live in California, while Gideon was living in New York. "A part of this virtual company thing was an experiment," Gideon noted. "We felt that technology had moved so rapidly that we could use the latest electronic meeting and communication techniques to tie everybody in and be effective. But, frankly, the management team was stretched."

No one was stretched more than Gideon. "Ask some of my girlfriends when I was working all night or traveling," he said. He was shuttling back and forth to Boston, schmoozing clients all over the country, flying to sales meetings, and, of course, participating in Giga's conferences, all the while shooting off emails and making cross-country telephone calls to David to try to keep Giga's explosive growth on track.

This wasn't the way it was supposed to be. Gideon had made it clear that he didn't want to run the day-to-day operations. "But I could not find a CEO. I looked, but could not find one whom I trusted. So I retained the CEO title and the board agreed to hire a Chief Operating Officer, a COO, who would be the CEO-elect."

It didn't work out in practice. Over the years, Giga went through three COOs. Meanwhile, quality and productivity suffered. "When you grow as fast as we were growing, you're not as rigorous in terms of who you hire as perhaps you should be," Gideon explained. "Sales productivity may go down from that perspective. You have training obligations that perhaps are more than you can handle as a small company."

But Giga had very steep sales objectives to achieve Gideon's growth targets. One COO felt that such high objectives were counterproductive; falling short on sales goals could cause morale to weaken. Gideon felt that the shortfall was a fault in operations and said: "Why don't you have better training in place? From an operational perspective, perhaps *you're* not doing a good enough job."

Philosophical Differences

Gideon's plans for Giga's growth became an issue, then a sticking point, and, ultimately, the cause of an irrefutable and fundamental difference in philosophy between him and the board of directors. Fueling the rapid and extensive expansion required money, and Giga was running through cash at a rapid rate.

It was clear that going public would be the cheapest way to fund the growth of the company. There had been discussion of an investment from Allen & Company, but the terms were far more limiting than a public offering. Gideon said, "The board felt that going public was the best thing to do." And so Giga went public in July of 1998, despite a shaky stock market plagued by Asian debt crises.

Giga's stock, which sold for $12 $\frac{1}{2}$ in the July IPO, crashed to $2 $\frac{3}{4}$ in October. Although it recovered to $6 $\frac{5}{8}$ by January 1999 (by which time the entire market had temporarily re-stabilized) the company had burned through a breathtaking $54 million[12] and Giga's board of directors turned gun-shy.

"That was the beginning of the end," Gideon said.

"We had too many directors too soon. I wrote emails and I visited with them," Gideon recalled. "I said, 'You're making a major mistake because just by slowing the growth, the growth is going to disappear. There's a growth culture in the company already. Even though we've fallen short of our objectives, look at how fast we're growing. Just extend the revenue and the cost lines, and we will be profitable before the end of 1999." (As it turned out, Giga became profitable very soon, at the end of 2000.) The huge board, most of whom rarely attended meetings, refused to acknowledge Giga's significant growth. Gideon immediately stepped down as CEO.

During the next few years, Gideon thought of trying to buy back the company – he remained, after all, the largest shareholder – "so I could bring it back to where I thought it ought to be," he said. The effort was unsuccessful. "At that point, I was out of the business," he said.

Then, too, the business climate had shifted. The super-heated tech bubble of the late 1990s had fizzled after the frenzied ramp-up to

_____

12 "Former Giga Head Gideon Gartner Explains His Exit." Boston Globe, January 20, 1999. http://www.highbeam.com/doc/1P2-8535624.html

Y2K (as "year 2000" was called), and the new millennium brought challenges no one had dreamed of, especially with the terrorist attacks on the United States on September 11th, 2001. Amid the subsequent economic freeze, the info-tech advisory business shrank and consolidated as companies cut back their IT research to just two or three providers.

With the future of the company in question, Giga's board of directors decided that if it could sell the company, it should sell the company. As the news became known that Giga was for sale, Forrester Research expressed an interest in buying it. The deal seemed to make sense: Forrester's research projected the major industry trends at a high level; Giga (like Gartner, but different) supplied the nuts and bolts of what IT installations and organizations required to help them accomplish their day-to-day business. Many of Giga's 900 clients were in government and financial services, sectors where Forrester fell short. Furthermore, Giga's research was geared toward IT executives, rather than marketers, a distinction that was hoped would help it weather the slowdown.[13] Forrester offered $60 million, in cash.

"It was an incredible deal for Forrester and was a good deal for the Giga shareholders because it was a multiple of where the stock price was at the time," Gideon noted. The announcement was made on January 21, 2003. Giga was out of business. It was time to move on.

---

13 "Forrester Grabs Giga As Research Sector Shrinks," InternetNews.com, January 21, 2003.

Gideon playing piano in his Manhattan home;
at left are daughter Sabrina and son Perry;
at right is wife Sarah.

Chapter 14: Gideon's Passions

The values that enabled Gideon to succeed in business – over and over and over – are the same values he has used to guide him in all aspects of his life: his insatiable curiosity, his brilliant analytical mind, his close connection to his family, his deep love of music, his fundamental sense of fairness, his constant quest for improvement in every system (including his own self), and his desire to share his ideas and enthusiasms.

When Gideon is enthusiastic about something – arts or activities, an educational cause or exploring a scientific concept – he supports it generously. The top ten recipients of his charitable giving over the past dozen years demonstrate his broad and eclectic range of interests. Those beneficiaries include, in order of the magnitude of his gifts:

- **Aspen Music Festival and School**

- **Opera Orchestra of New York**

- **The Aspen Institute**

- **Mount Sinai Medical Center** (supporting the research of Dr. Sam Gandy, head of Alzheimer's research)

- **Carnegie Hall**

- **Metropolitan Opera**

- **Aspen Art Museum**

- **CLAL, The National Jewish Center for Learning and Leadership**

- **Jazz at Aspen Snowmass**

- **MIT**

Nor does he limit himself to major institutions. A true entrepreneur, Gideon often spots a spark of talent in smaller organizations and helps nurture it. He regularly contributes to many other groups, among them, these:

- **Manhattan Theatre Club**

- **All Hands Volunteers**

- **IT History Society**

- **New York City Center**

- **Richard Tucker Music Foundation**

- **Aspen Santa Fe Ballet**

- **New York Philharmonic**

- **The National Jazz Museum of Harlem**

- **New York Gilbert & Sullivan Players**

- **Yeshiva of Flatbush**

- **Anderson Ranch Arts Foundation**

In addition, Gideon appreciates beauty in both intellectual and physical forms, as evidenced by his collection of fine art, his joy of outdoor activities, especially in the pure thrill of a powder day on the ski slopes of Colorado, Utah and Switzerland, a laser-targeted backhand in tennis, and his fascination with the strategy behind a good game of chess. And, of course, he has always dedicated himself to furthering the progress of his birth country, Israel.

Gideon feels strongly that to be a successful entrepreneur, one has to have passion for the world – not just for one's own limited industry. He hopes that these words might inspire young entrepreneurs of the next generation to broaden their scope and throw themselves into intellectual and creative endeavors beyond the limits of an MBA.

A true entrepreneur needs to be above all a well-rounded person, thick-skinned and iron-willed, with a wealth of family and friends to pick him up when he is down and to join the celebrations when he is up. Gideon is a man of many talents, but above all, he has a talent for living life to the fullest — and he hopes that by relating these steps and missteps of his journey, he can continue to be a helpful guide to the youth of tomorrow.

Afterwords by Friends and Family

FAMILY, BUSINESS, CULTURE, PHILANTHROPY, ART, SPORTS AND NATURE – these passions have made Gideon Gartner a well-rounded man of hidden depths, serving him well in business. As friends and family from the full spectrum of his life testify in these subsequent pages, Gideon Gartner is a man much admired, listened to, and loved in every aspect of his life.

A Constant Stream of Ideas

"You can't sit with Gideon for more than 10 minutes without him proposing an idea."

Neill Brownstein
Co-founder, Bessemer Venture Partners and Footprint Ventures

Many people who start companies have big egos, and that's not bad – in fact, that's usually a good thing. Ego drives people to achievement. With Gideon's first company – Gartner Group – there was no mistaking that it was his company. The same with his second company – GIGA incorporates his own initials: <u>Gi</u>deon <u>Ga</u>rtner.

But success for Gideon doesn't necessarily mean enormous amount of money. He's not driven by wealth but rather by playing a leading part in changing the world. Seeing his ideas come to fruition was what his success meant to him. The fact that the Gartner Group business model is still working well gives Gideon a tremendous amount of personal pride, satisfaction and accomplishment. It's the same with his personal interests. He derives a lot of satisfaction identifying organizations aligned with his personal interests and giving them a little nudge up the hill. He gets satisfaction out of following his heart.

The most outstanding aspect of Gideon's personality is his boyish, unadulterated enthusiasm for ideas. It's literally an effervescence of ideas. You can't sit with Gideon for more than ten minutes without him proposing an idea or delivering a critique.

One of his ideas had to do with improving a standard conference table with a device enabling people sitting around the table to vote anonymously. That way, whether the vote was 9-0 or 5-4, the idea was to have an electronic system so that people didn't have to divulge how they were voting, and therefore result in a true and unbiased vote. Today, people can vote on the web anonymously. As with so many things, it turns out that Gideon was ahead of the times. His was a wacky idea then, but is *de rigueur* today.

There's another story about Gideon that not too many people know. As you read in this book, we did the napkin deal outlining the structure of Gartner Group Story and we were ready to roll in March of 1978. But we didn't close the deal until September 1979 – 18 months later. The reason was that Gideon felt it wasn't a good enough deal – not for him, but for the other people he was bringing in at the beginning. He said, "It's not a fair deal. You've got to include more stock for other people." He nudged it along until we made a better deal for management – 70/30 for management. And the company never needed more money.

Would I say that Gideon is a *mensch?* Definitely.

A Congenial Dreamer who Got the Job Done

"While Gideon is a dreamer, he's very strong inside. He has lots of intellectual rigor."

Charley Ellis

Former member of Gartner Group board of directors

Gideon and I first crossed paths without seeing one another, let alone knowing one another, when his firm and my firm happened to make simultaneous offers to purchase some real estate in Greenwich, Connecticut. Gideon's firm was turned down, because it was not judged to be as credit-worthy as my firm. (This was back in the early days of Gartner Group.) Being intrigued, Gideon wondered, "Who are these guys?" So he called and asked, "Who are you?" I said, "I'm Charley Ellis." "No, no," he said. "What does your company do?" I told him that we were a research-based consulting firm serving the financial world. Gideon said, "That's interesting. *We're* a research-based consulting firm serving the technology world. We should get together and compare notes. Maybe we should do some of the things you do, and maybe you should do some of what we do." So we got together and we immediately hit it off.

We stayed in touch and a few years later, Gideon called again. He said, "I'd like you to come over and get to know my company because I think you might like to be a director." So for a few years in the early 1980s, I was a director at Gartner Group. I enjoyed it tremendously. The firm had a lift-off characteristic such that if you were any kind of observer, you thought, "This has lots of potential."

At board meetings, Gideon had a nice quality of sincerity as well as irreverence for anything like a structured, formal process. He was always looking to get insight or understanding or even pushback, so he could see more clearly what might be the right thing to do. I often asked challenging questions, and several times I honestly thought I was going too far, but afterwards Gideon always said, "You know, I wish you'd been tougher in asking your questions."

The truth is, that while Gideon is a dreamer, he's very strong inside. He has lots of intellectual rigor. He can take any kind of discussion to a very high level – if you're able to keep up with him. He's always striving to get it right.

It's unusual that someone who is really congenial and fun to be with is also very focused on excellence of analysis, excellence of results, on trying to create an excellent organization. It was great fun watching him in the process of creating and constantly recreating Gartner Group. Because the firm didn't start off the way it developed; it kept changing and morphing. I always enjoyed watching that.

Gideon's a very, very enjoyable person to be with. The name itself symbolizes something uplifting and positive, and his manner is so extraordinarily engaging, so very friendly and outgoing and warm. And he has beautiful eyes, a wonderful smile, and he laughs quickly and warmly.

One of my favorite Gideon episodes took place when my wife and I responded to his invitation to visit in Aspen. It was a joy to see him.

(I hadn't seen him for a year.) He said, "Charley, everyone should do something once in a while that's mind-changing, circumstance-changing, uplifting and thrilling. I've taken my own advice, and I've decided to do that. When I was a kid I used to play piano, and I was pretty good. There's a magnificent piano instructor here in Aspen – so mind-blowing, so capable. We've been working together a couple of hours a day, advancing my skills. I'd like to play for you."

I said, "Gee, Gideon, I'd love to listen to you play. Is this going to be show tunes?" Gideon scoffed, "Are you kidding? This is serious music, Chopin." I said, "That's really hard." Gideon responded, "It *is* quite hard, but I have one piece I've completely mastered. Let me play it for you."

He sat down at his beautiful piano and started playing. At first, he was quite gentle but as the piece became more demanding, he became more deeply involved: His hands were moving back and forth, his body swaying back and forth, his head also, with his hair flying around. It was thrilling to watch this wonderful guy be able to play such a difficult piece, and it looked as though it took everything he had.

When he finished, he rested for a minute. Then he said, "Would you like me to play some more?" I said, "Sure." He stood up and the piano started to play by itself. It turned out to be a player piano! How many people do you know who could do something like that, just for the fun of it? And the fun of it was terrific.

I think his conceptualizing capabilities are way under-estimated. At IBM, his abilities to understand the computer industry were very advanced. At Oppenheimer, he was even more in front of understanding both the computer industry and investments in it. He did it again at Gartner Group. Serial creativity in different environments is very unusual, but I understand that's quite normal for him.

If Gideon were a composer, he would be Charles Ives. Think about it: Ives was a genius in the life insurance industry when it was just getting started. He was the number two officer at New York Life Insurance and invented all sorts of life insurance products; he was a very skilled quantitative analyst who could figure out what people wanted and make it work. But that's only one dimension. In another dimension, he was a composer, although with some few exceptions, none of his pieces was performed during his lifetime. Certainly, the NY Philharmonic and the Boston Symphony never performed his works until after he had died. But he wasn't composing to please others; he was doing it to figure out his theories about music.

Similarly, there will always be a mad scientist in Gideon. I suspect that if you gave him a choice between either making all the money you can imagine or doing all the creative work you want to do, it wouldn't take him a nanosecond to decide. He'd take Number Two.

The Grand Strategist

"If Gideon were an operatic figure, he would be Figaro. He's a grand strategist."

Stewart Greenfield
Co-founder Oak Investment Partners;
Board member, Opera Orchestra of NY

Gideon and I first met at IBM in 1965. I was running IBM's first experiment in dark marketing data. Gideon had just returned from Israel and I tried to recruit him into our organization. As it was, he went into the Commercial Analysis Department, which probably was the better route for him since it gave him the training that likely led to the formation of Gartner Group.

We had grown somewhat friendly and when he was hired by E.F. Hutton, he invited me to New York to talk about life on Wall Street and the possibility of my going down there. He got me focused in that direction. It's because of Gideon that I went into venture capital, rather than company research.

Gideon dotes on music, and his business success enabled him to indulge himself: to go to opera in many places in the world, to host cocktail parties for the Opera Orchestra of New York (OONY), and to buy his beloved Bösendorfer piano.

Gideon is a superb analyst and critic of opera. My wife and I would go to an opera with Gideon and then we'd discuss what was wrong and how it could have been better. He always had a great number of comments to make.

About fifteen or twenty years ago, Gideon invited my wife and me to a performance of the Opera Orchestra of New York. We enjoyed it and started subscribing to its performances. In the late 1990s, Gideon recruited me to join its board. He eventually brought a couple of other people in to serve on the board, people who also became significant contributors to OONY. The performances provide a little more than a quarter of the cost of maintaining the organization, so contributions were critical.

About four years ago, in the wake of the financial crisis and the Great Recession, OONY, along with virtually every cultural organization in the US, faced contribution levels that were tailing off. Endowments had contracted and individuals weren't making as much money as they used to. So OONY fell into a period of stress. A sharp division formed in the board between those members who were concerned with continuing the old way of doing things and those who were concerned about the survival of the orchestra.

Gideon led the contingent that was focused on keeping the orchestra in a position to provide performances, albeit at a reduced schedule. Along with bringing in new people and new ideas, Gideon strongly argued for a succession plan for Eve Queler, OONY's founder. It was particularly difficult to get contributors enthused, when there was the possibility that the OONY might disappear if Eve stepped down. But Gideon strongly urged that appointing a junior conductor to provide visible continuity would be a critical step. He argued for a conductor who was in New York and affiliated with a university. His suggestion was implemented with the appointment of Italian conductor Alberto Veronesi, who, in addition to being a good conductor, had some strong supporters among the wealthy Italians who made contributions to the OONY. That helped OONY survive.

If Gideon were an operatic figure, I would nominate him for the role of Figaro. Like Figaro, he's a grand strategist.

Birds of a Feather

"Over the years I've known him, Gideon has always had ideas for new businesses. It's a constant theme."

Judith Hamilton
Former CEO of Dataquest;
Former CEO of Classroom Connect;
Former CEO of First Floor Software;
Member of The Presidents Roundtable

I was introduced to Gideon in 1990 by my ex-husband, who was also an analyst. At the time, I was running Dataquest. Gideon had already left Gartner but I was very interested in meeting him because he had revolutionized that type of business. My impressions were, as they have remained, that he's a very intelligent, thoughtful, and kind person.

Shortly thereafter, I was asked to join the Presidents Roundtable, of which Gideon was already a member. The Roundtable grew out of a trade organization, the Association of Data Processing Software and Service Companies, which held two conferences per year. The Association also supported "birds of a feather" meetings around the conferences; the Roundtable started as a "birds of the feather" meeting where CEOs of software/services companies could discuss issues from the point of view of being CEOs in the same industry.

Over time, those meetings separated from the trade organization and were held on their own. The format was – and remains – that each person gets a block of time to discuss any issues which that person wants. In the early years, the issues were almost always business-related. In later years, they could be anything from new businesses or new interests to personal problems with children or health. Anything the person wants to talk about is allowed and the other people act as a personal board of directors, offering insight and information with the person as the primary recipient, not their company or shareholders. Everyone pays diligent attention to everyone else and tries to give the best advice possible.

Gideon's role is one of equals in the Roundtable. He gives advice to people, as does everyone. He's a very good listener. He tends to be on the quiet side, and he's always taking notes, either about his own upcoming presentation or about what the person who is speaking says. He's very sympathetic and gives thoughtful advice.

Over the years I've known him, Gideon has always had ideas for new businesses. It's been a constant theme. Almost all of his ideas revolve around the same field as the original Gartner Group: analysis and information in the world of technology made available in new and different and specific ways.

Although a couple of people have left the group and a couple of people have been added, the Roundtable is basically the same group of people. But there's definitely a difference in interests. Everyone used to be software/services executives. Now one person runs a charity to aid people who have been through natural disasters, one person is writing mystery novels, and one has largest collection of medieval manuscripts in the world. The personality of the group has stayed the same, though. We're all the same age, so we're facing the same issues that come with aging, so we discuss health now more than we used to.

Gideon is no different, though. His interests are always new businesses – how to implement new businesses.

Gideon just doesn't want to not be in the game. That's why he continues to have all these great ideas. He was champing at the bit when we first met – and he's doing it even now. His idea-a-minute for a new business is not just a passing thought; he spends enormous amounts of time fleshing out his ideas and presenting them. Sometimes it results in a company, like Giga or Gartner, and sometimes it doesn't get that far.

He enjoys the implementation of his ideas. He likes to see them actually take shape and be used in business. That matters a lot to him. So the fruition of ideas through the establishment of a company is very important to him.

Because Gideon is best-known for his business activities, people don't realize how very thoughtful and kind he is. In my experience, Gideon always follows up and checks in on me, based on whatever I'm dealing with. If I miss a meeting of the Roundtable, it's always Gideon who calls to see how I am.

One of my favorite memories of Gideon is of the time a group of us were out walking around and Gideon and several others bought ice cream cones. Gideon ate several bites and then threw it away. I asked why. He said, *"Because I've eaten all I've wanted."* That struck me as a wise statement – that you don't have to eat all of the ice cream cone.

Gideon's Love of Music

"Gideon has always been a very involved audience member. He can speak knowledgeably about different performers, different interpretations – and there's no lack of opinions."

Nadine Asin
Flutist and faculty member, Aspen Music Festival

I'm a flutist and have been an artist and faculty member on the board of the Aspen Music Festival since 1978. That's how I met Gideon. He was a lay member of the board, one of the 39 lay members invited to serve by the nominating committee. (The eleven other members are elected artist/faculty members.)

My initial impression was and remains how extremely knowledgeable and passionate Gideon is about classical music. It really is a great passion of his. He can speak knowledgeably about different performers, different interpretations – and there's no lack of opinions.

At board meetings, he had no problem asking the provocative question. Once, for a brief moment, the Aspen Festival was considering presenting visiting orchestras. It was a controversial idea that would change the structure of the Festival. As a faculty member, that didn't appeal to me, but Gideon insisted on an in-depth discussion. And he was right: You have to make a judgment based on all the facts. The conclusion was that visiting orchestras were not something the Festival was prepared to move ahead with. What struck me afterwards was that my first reaction was totally subjective; his reaction was objective. That's what made him a great businessman.

Through our membership on the board, I came to know Gideon as a friend. I used to play at the Metropolitan Opera in the wintertime, and it was at the opening performance of "Das Rheingold" that my husband proposed to me. Gideon had asked me to get him tickets for one of the performances and, as it happened, it was that one. He was the first person we saw after the performance when he came to thank me for getting him the ticket and he was the first person we told the news to. That's a special memory. And when he and Sarah became engaged, we were all at a party and I dragged them over to where my husband and I were standing so we could celebrate together.

Gideon has always been a very involved audience member. As a performer, I like to look out and see my people in the house. With Gideon, I didn't have to look too far. I knew exactly where to look. He always sat in the front row at the Aspen Festival, and continues to do so at Carnegie Hall and the Metropolitan Opera – or within the first three rows. And I understand why he wants to sit up there: He wants to be as close to the performance as possible.

We always talk about new productions at the Met and our discussions get pretty erudite. After one performance, Gideon had to go home and watch another production on DVD of the same opera that he had just seen, just to compare the two. That's the kind of unending curiosity he has.

We have occasionally played piano-flute duets together. He's terrific as a partner. He was very excited when he acquired the silver-legged turquoise 9 ½ -foot Bösendorfer piano designed by Porsche. It had taken over a year to build. There were certain aspects that disappointed him; it had a different action and different sound from a Steinway. I'd never seen such a beautiful piano before. Our christening duet was by Debussy.

Gideon is endlessly interested in things. He is very naturally curious and bright and involved, and that's what makes him so interesting to be around. You know you're not going be allowed to sit back and take anything for granted.

He's a traditional guy for all of his forward thinking. He loves to celebrate the Jewish holidays, he likes to celebrate his birthday. I remember a Passover seder where Sarah had prepared an alternate *haggadah*. At a certain point, Gideon just looked at it and said, "What *is* this?" He had a whole different idea of what a *haggadah* should be. And Sarah graciously said, "Okay, let's do it your way."

I think he has tremendous pride – and justifiably so – of his business accomplishments. He doesn't use his money as a bully pulpit. But he has strong opinions and he's a very bright man, so his opinions are quite specific and he's got a way of thinking that people otherwise wouldn't come across.

I think that he has a very big heart. He uses it to the benefit of many wonderful organizations.

In the world of classical music, he's been very involved with different organizations and been tremendously generous and genuinely helpful. He cares deeply about the continuation and development of the art form.

If Gideon were a composer, I would see him as an amalgam. He has the intellectual, rational side of Bach, he has the high romantic side of Brahms, and he certainly has the breadth of Brahms. And then he has the meticulousness in his thinking of Beethoven. However, in my opinion, Gideon's one flaw is that he does not like Mozart. I'm doing my best to get him over this imperfection.

Crossing Swords as an Art Form

"Gideon is so smart and so able that losing an argument to him was a pleasure."

Leon Botstein
Musician and President, Bard College

I first met Gideon in Aspen. The main subject of our interaction was Gideon's idea for revising the way program notes were written. I thought, "Here is an enthusiastic, committed, discerning music lover who is concerned about the future of the audience and wants to do something to ensure a healthy future of this art form."

He wanted to see whether we could be a vehicle by which his new formula for program notes could be tried out. I was absolutely enthusiastic about his interest in revising the typical format, although I disagreed with his approach. However, it was certainly worth a try because he might be right and I might be wrong. We had a lot of arguments about it. We also argued about concerts we had both heard.

Gideon is an extremely engaging person to argue with. I enjoyed crossing swords with him, so much so that I always took the opportunity to contradict him. I enjoyed that and he did too. I especially enjoyed my failure to persuade him to change his mind. He's so smart and so able that losing an argument to him was a pleasure.

Although ultimately his idea for program notes didn't work for us at Bard, the great thing was that Gideon was deeply, emotionally engaged in the art form of classical music. It was a pleasure to see him get all worked up and excited about a piece of music or an aspect of a performance. It was a genuine pleasure. It was also frustrating because the right thing to do in fund-raising was to agree with him, but he was too intelligent to flatter.

If Gideon were a piece of music, he would be a brilliant virtuosic etude that reveals glimpses of genius in improvisation but is unfinished. It would be filled with ideas, flashes of brilliance, surprises, unexpected twists and turns. That's how I would describe Gideon: A piece of music with no filler or boring sections, never treading water, always engaging; a very fast piece of music, not contemplative or sad, and always with a sparkle.

Revolutionizing Program Notes

"Gideon immediately saw the potential. Gideon is enormously smart."

Bob Martin
Director, Conservatory of Music at Bard College

I first met Gideon through Mortimer and Mimi Levitt. I've known them a long time through the Young Concert Artists and they are dear friends of Gideon and Sarah.

We started the Conservatory in 2005. You can imagine, when starting a new school, it's great for the students to have a chance to perform and to make new friends. One of the wonderful things that Gideon and Sarah did was host a concert in their apartment with 50 to 60 people. We had students, violinists, woodwinds, singers – it was one of our first and most exciting house concerts and a showcase event for the Conservatory. Gideon and Sarah even had a photographer there. It was a big morale boost.

Early on, Gideon told me about his idea for how to improve the concert experience through better program notes. The usual experience is that you sit down, socialize with friends, and open up Playbill, only to be confronted by a long essay that you have to search all through to learn about the music. Gideon had the idea that there would be sections – modules, as he called them – on everything: the instrumentation, facts about the composer, etc. He showed me some samples and I thought it was a great idea.

At a music school like Bard, with a new Conservatory, this could be something for our students; they could work on the modules and assemble them in advance to have on hand. Our Conservatory is unusual. It's a five-year double-degree program; in addition to a music degree, students get a BA in a field not related to music. Obviously there's an emphasis on students being well-educated, and Gideon immediately saw the potential for his program notes to be a vehicle for enhancing the education of the students. I thought it was wonderful.

So we started. Our idea was that students would write the program notes and be paid a small honorarium. Gideon gave some initial gifts to help us get going. His idea was that this could become a revenue source for us – that we could have program notes available to other orchestras, and sell it.

Unfortunately, we were not able to make it work in any way he had hoped. The reason was pretty simple: It became clear that ensuring that the concert program note modules were at a high quality level required supervision from the faculty and time commitment from the students. Both then and now, students are extraordinarily busy. Just consider someone trying to become a world-class concert artist and at same time doing a second degree – trying to become a French major, for example. They didn't have the time to devote to it. Plus they have generous scholarships and a few hundred dollars wouldn't make a difference. And the faculty – this was a second job for them.

We did it for about two or three years. Gideon sent the notes to colleagues at the Aspen Music Festival, and the Festival people called us up and asked how we did it. It started off with a lot of enthusiasm on all sides, and I never doubted that he was on to a really good idea. But we could never make it quite work.

My favorite memory of Gideon is from the first time I went to see him at his apartment. I sat down in his office, and he was showing me what he had done, and I looked at a mock-up of the concert note modules, and I felt excitement – intellectual and entrepreneurial excitement. Gideon is enormously smart and it was thrilling to brainstorm with him. And talking about a new venture with a venture person like him was very satisfying. When someone like Gideon says, "You have a good idea," you feel pretty good about it.

That Renaissance Quality

"Gideon is like an idea tree."

Norman Raben
Chairman of the Board, Opera Orchestra of New York

I first met Gideon in 2007 at an Opera Orchestra of New York (OONY) board meeting. I'd been invited to attend the meeting as a guest. The board was making a decision about the future of OONY, and I was invited to discuss the options. At the end of the meeting, I was asked to join OONY as president and chairman.

I'm not sure Gideon made much of an impression then; there were a lot of people there, plus much conversation. Shortly thereafter, Gideon held a musical evening at his apartment. It was the first chance we got to talk and discuss music, OONY, and the entire artistic world. Gideon attracted me very quickly; he's got a very puckish quality and a quirky mind, and I've always been a sucker for quirky minds. He also has a renaissance quality – he's a guy who came out of the computer world and he plays the piano, patronizes the arts, and is well-rounded. We developed a friendship pretty rapidly.

OONY had been founded by Eve Queler to present beautiful but relatively unknown operas in concert form. The Metropolitan Opera tenor Richard Tucker had approached Eve forty years ago and offered to be our first star. The idea was to have a singer of Richard Tucker's caliber in a main role. (You need a name to bring people in the door.) During Eve's reign, virtually everyone of note sang with us: Nicolai Gedda, Placido Domingo, and now the Jonas Kaufmanns of the opera world are singing with us. Gideon was very much a part of supporting that.

Most of the focus of our early conversations was on the concept of opera in concert form. Gideon is a strong supporter of opera in concert form because he feels you get to focus on the music and singers, as opposed to being distracted by costumes and sets (not to mention the cost difference). Most of his comments focused on that area: how the singers were presented, the music stands, the notes for people to read. Gideon doesn't do things by half measures; he was very deeply involved. And the critiques? Trust me, the emails are always active.

Gideon also felt that we should push ahead into twentieth-century music as opposed to the bel canto repertoire that had been the mainstay of OONY over the years. He felt the world was changing and he was aggressive in his desire to move OONY into the modern music world. He was also very supportive of our transition from Eve Queler, our founder, to the hiring of our new music director, Alberto Veronesi, which allowed us to broaden our funding base as well as build relationships with today's generation of great singers.

Gideon is a fanatic art attendee. He and Sarah are always going to an opening or a performance. Gideon led me to some interesting venues that I didn't even know about. Gideon has catholic tastes, so he would drag me into the world of contemporary music.

Gideon is not a person who would write a check and sit back. He'd rather try to sell his ideas to the people who make decisions in an organization. I think his ideas about the arts are as important to him as the arts themselves.

Gideon is like an idea tree. One of my former partners, a fellow at MIT, was describing this mad scientist who was a professor emeritus at MIT. MIT assigned a team to be with this guy and as ideas streamed forth, their responsibility was to write them down and then decide which would make sense. Gideon is like that.

A big part of every chairman's job is managing the board members individually. I had a lot of contact with Gideon on a detailed level and I cherished the relationship. A friendship doesn't always have to mean agreeing with someone. It also means respecting and caring for someone. I just enjoy talking with Gideon.

Some of the moments I enjoyed most were at his apartment, when we brought in singers, musicians, and Gideon's friends. It's amazing how Gideon attracts friends. It was like a Parisian salon. There'd be all sorts of people from the worlds of arts and music, and a few techies. Then Gideon would have the urge to sit down at the piano and be part of the gig. Gideon was never the star of the evening; he would simply be the surprise cherry on top of the banana split.

A Man on the Move

"Plenty of CEOs are psychopaths, lack empathy or are manipulative. Gideon has fundamental decency."

Don Gartner
Gideon's younger brother

Gideon is a brainstormer. He does it on a professional and personal level. When you're a brainstormer, you throw out ideas, some of which are brilliant and incisive and others may be absolutely harebrained. Gideon's brainstorming extends to the most mundane things. If you wanted to go to a ballgame, or a restaurant, or anything – like go on a vacation – it would be hard to tie him down because there would be an eruption of thoughts and ideas, and always involved debate.

Another aspect of his personality is that Gideon can't stand the idea of wasting time. He would go to baseball games, because he didn't perceive that as wasting time, but he won't read fiction, because he can't see a purpose to it.

In the summer of 1967, just after my senior year in college, I came back home and Gideon went with me to buy a used car. I was 22 and Gideon was 32. We went to a dealership in Queens. Gideon saw the salesman we were dealing with in his partitioned office and the salesman was studying a thick manual. Gideon commented favorably on it: "This guy is on the ball, he is studying his field."

That indicated the way Gideon liked to spend his time, whether he was playing chess or the piano or engaged in an intellectually demanding activity. There were leisure activities he accepted because they involved achieving a standard of skill. He had some appreciation for sports; when I was a kid, he would take me to Knicks and Rangers games. He was a good stickball player and we would play in the schoolyard across the street from our house. But reading a mystery or studying a baseball statistic – to him, that was screwing around.

Similarly, he couldn't sit still or stay on the phone with you for more than fifteen seconds. But that has changed now that he's gotten older.

In business, Gideon played in fast company and he excelled. Business success gave Gideon a whole range of accomplishments: a sense of achievement, a sense of recognition, the excitement and satisfaction of developing a new industry. How many people can say that they not only founded a company but did so in an area where nothing existed before?

I think Gideon is an honorable person. Everyone has personal peccadilloes; plenty of CEOs are psychopaths, lack empathy or are manipulative. With Gideon, there's an overarching sensibility. Gideon has fundamental decency.

Work Hard, Play Hard

"Gideon wants to learn everything about whatever he is interested in."

Perry Gartner
Gideon's son

More than almost anyone I know, Gideon fosters personal relationships with people he encounters in professional ways. His physicians almost always become people he socializes with outside of treatment. The same with lawyers whom he's had to retain. People who started off as professional acquaintances frequently become close friends.

He's very taken by people who are original, creative, and perhaps a bit eccentric. He likes to introduce them or use them as examples or role models. For example, in 1991, he was in Japan on a business trip and he invited me along. After meetings, he and I spent time exploring. We'd heard that there were boat tours along a historic river near Tokyo and there was an incredible rock garden we could visit at the end of the tour. We looked around for the pier where the boats started from but we just couldn't find it. Eventually, we walked over to a dinghy where an old Japanese gentleman was puttering around. We pointed to the map and tried to make ourselves understood and he tried to explain where we should be going but nothing was getting communicated.

He finally motioned for us to follow him and led us through a maze of streets, easily for a half-mile, to a point where he pointed to where we wanted to go. Then he waved, turned around and began walking back to his boat. Gideon was just flabbergasted; an elderly gent, clearly in the middle of his own work, had dropped everything to help out complete strangers. He referred to it on a number of occasions, as an example of how to behave and reach out to people.

Gideon embodied the work hard/play hard cliché. He worked exceedingly hard – and his work ethic was almost intimidating. Yet there was always room for intense participation in any number of extra-curricular pursuits: his own music, cultural events, constantly striving for self-improvement.

Gideon wants to learn everything about whatever he's interested in – and his interests are varied, whether it is chess, which he learned as a kid, or games he encountered later, like backgammon or go, or skiing or tennis. He doesn't just want to play them; he wants to master them and he studies them intensively. He wouldn't be satisfied with just playing the occasional game of tennis; he would take lessons regularly and study videos. It wasn't enough to go on a day's ski outing to Hunter Mountain. He'd organize a whole trip, beginning with instructional sessions with ski pros. Then he'd make a point to work on the specific techniques they were teaching him, and then he'd pass those techniques down to us on family ski trips.

Gideon feels that with wealth also comes responsibility. He feels it's important to have a robust philanthropic roster.

Gideon has a reputation, especially in management circles, for being difficult to work with because his demands can be extreme and his standards impossibly high. I actually think that he's much more self-effacing and honest than that characterization would lead you to expect.

He's constantly playing down his own smarts and intelligence. He'll refer to other colleagues as being far smarter than he is. If he's being interviewed for a conference, he's very quick to give others credit and to describe the process that led to certain things in a way that's really free of an agenda. And he's willing to apologize when he's wrong.

One of my favorite stories: We were on a family trip to England, when I was sixteen, and my sisters were fifteen and eleven. We were in London, eating at a Chinese restaurant in Soho. I mistakenly ate a red-hot pepper. I went nuts. I was making a terrible scene because my head was on fire. It was a nice restaurant – my dad was trying to introduce us to different aspects of multicultural cuisine – and it was embarrassing for him. He was saying, "Perry, you're making a scene, I know it's uncomfortable, but you have to stop it." Finally, he said, "Perry, I'm going to eat one right now, so you can see how to deal with it even if it's uncomfortable." So he ate one. And he turned all shades of red, and punched his hand into his chest, and grabbed for the water. When he could speak again, he said, "I'm sorry, Perry. You were right."

Throughout the Gartner Group years, I always knew superficially what Gideon did for a living. I knew that he was successful. But it wasn't until I went to work at Giga in 1996 – I was there for four-and-a-half years, heading up their competitive analysis division – that I began to realize who he really was and how others responded to him. At industry events or with a clients, invariably the reactions of people when they found out Gideon was my father were completely surreal. I knew him as my dad, and a tough act to follow. But I wasn't aware of the degree to which he was seen as a demigod rock star in the industry. It was *holy cow* amazement – and big-time pride.

Down to Earth and Kind

*"Gideon truly enjoys sharing his experiences and
creative ideas with other people in order to help
them, particularly those launching or running
young, ambitious ventures of their own."*

Sabrina Gartner
Gideon's daughter

My father's business success means that he is a success in his
father's eyes. My grandfather was a very disciplined, serious man
who immigrated to the U.S. from Eastern Europe and considered
education and work paramount to being able to live a valued life in
this country. While he was a successful civil engineer, he did not
achieve success on the scale that my father did. So when the
headquarters of Gartner Group, an impressive campus and
building complex, was built in Greenwich, CT, my grandfather
wept with pride upon visiting it soon after its opening. I'm sure
nothing could have made my father feel more validated and
content, and happy that he had made his father happy.

An important aspect of what Gideon enjoys as a result of his
success is having a voice that is heard. He truly enjoys sharing his
experiences and creative ideas with other people in order to help
them, particularly those launching or running young, ambitious
ventures of their own. He has more time now to influence others in
whom he believes, and to help them exploit their visions using his

vision, risk-taking, smart business planning and willingness to be a fierce negotiator in order to make things happen.

My father feels that with wealth also comes philanthropic responsibility. His deep-seeded interest in Jewish history and culture and education – fundamental interests instilled in him by his father – shows in his ongoing commitment to these causes through charitable contributions. Gideon did not grow up in a family that had access to such financial choices, yet, he has made it a priority for himself. I believe my father does this because he wants to, not because he should, or is expected to, and because he cares on a personal level as someone who identifies with the plight of people.

My father has a brilliant creative brain, this is well-known. But only those lucky enough to be acquainted with him on a personal level know that he has an impish, fanciful side that is tolerant of people of all colors and personalities. He would just as soon – and often prefers to – go out to eat at a local greasy spoon as at a three-star restaurant. And he'd ride the subway to get there.

As fiercely competitive as he is in all aspects of business, he also is just as happy, if not happier, when the person he's playing chess with wins – although this doesn't happen often. He has achieved a certain position in life but often you'll hear those who meet him describe him as "down to earth" and "such a nice guy."

During the Gartner years, while he was still a bachelor, he lived in Westport, Connecticut. He hired a houseman to take care of the property, cook and drive him to work and to the airport, as he was constantly traveling. But the real reason for hiring him had nothing to do with the luxury aspect of it; instead it had everything to do with wanting to have as much time as possible to work and concentrate on building the business. Being driven to work – a twenty-minute affair – was not a time to sit back and relax for Gideon; it meant he'd have a few more minutes to get some more work done in the back seat.

The houseman was a professional and wanted to treat Gideon like a king, which, for example, meant when he picked Gideon up from the office to drive him to JFK Airport, he wanted to carry Gideon's bags out of the office for him. But Gideon would never let him. He was too humble and did not want to convey the wrong message about himself to his staff. He would never let anyone see that someone else was carrying his bags – and they were extremely heavy, with all his paperwork! – out of the office to the chauffeured car.

I had worked summers at Gartner Group ever since its inception in 1979, when there were just a handful of us in a relatively small rented office space in downtown Greenwich, Connecticut, to when we moved into the large corporate headquarters. After Gideon launched Giga Information Group, my brother Perry and I worked there for several years; I was involved with the marketing end of things, eventually becoming director of corporate communications, and Perry worked in sales and competitive analysis. I can say that there was never any nepotism shown to us with respect to what we did; in fact, things were sometimes made more difficult for me by Gideon in an effort to show that we were not receiving special treatment. Working for Gideon was serious business and it was always fun! Both companies employed the best young brains around, so the office environment was always buzzing with excitement and challenge.

What I remember most fondly from Gartner Group was when Gideon chose the stalking horse as a symbol for the company's business practices. At Gartner, "stalking horse" was a phrase describing a research tool used by research analysts for proving and defending their findings. It was around then that Gideon commissioned me to produce a painting entitled "Stalking Horse." He had the painting hung in his office, which meant the world to me, more than any position I achieved or any work I did at the company. This eventually led to subsequent painting commissions by the company for other "Gartner paintings" with title phrases such as "Straw Man" (another research phrase/tool).

It was an honor not only to be a member of the vital workforce at both Gartner and Giga, but to see my own paintings hang in the hallways and offices because my father wanted them there. This meant everything to me but it is one of the most important aspects about my father and who he is. He is proud of his business but he is also proud of his family.

A Love of Beauty

"His exuberance for everything in life is something I'm very proud of. It's contagious and makes everyone want to be with him."

Aleba Gartner
Gideon's daughter

All my life I've been aware of my father's style, humor, talent, and intellect. His appreciation for originality, novelty and greatness is ever-present, as is his instinct to figure out how to make something good even better.

Even as a young girl, I knew how much he admired the Japanese as inventors of functional, cutting-edge, and beautiful design. The first calculator he ever gave me, in first or second grade, was a paper-thin Sharp with a flat surface and no buttons. I was so excited to bring it to school and show my friends this amazing futuristic-looking machine. Later on, his love for Japanese design became manifest in his clothing, for example Issey Miyake's stunning fabrics, folds, and colors. My father didn't dress like other dads, and he also didn't drive cars like anyone. His sports cars were often the only one of their kind on the road — I don't know how he found them. One was a burgundy Triumph Stag in the late 1970s, a convertible, and he'd let us kids perch on top of the back seat – the three of us just barely fit – while he drove around. I used to feel a flush of embarrassment when we'd slow down to approach a tollbooth, since opera would be blasting on the radio. We must have made an unusual picture, but no question, it was always exciting and extra-special to have him take us out.

I knew that my father worked very, very hard during the day, though I never understood exactly what it was he did, other than it had to do with technology. I was more aware of the fact that when he came home, the first thing he did was go to the piano and play the most beautiful music I had ever heard. Chopin, Schumann, Bach… he'd pour out his heart and make funny faces that were unintentional. I loved to listen and watch.

When I grew a bit older, I realized how lucky we were to have our father take us to concerts at Carnegie Hall and operas at the Met. But he was quite serious about instilling in us a love and appreciation for great music. He would often have us listen at home, first to whatever piece was going to be performed, so that we could enjoy and understand it more. My gift upon graduating from college was a subscription to the entire San Francisco Ring Cycle. Along with this gift was a suggestion that I attend lectures and demonstrations at the Wagner Society, and read a book or two on the music and symbolism of Wagner's Ring. I was easily the youngest at these Society gatherings, and I still have my notes and the articles they distributed. My dad was right – I would not have fully appreciated the fifteen-hour Ring Cycle without all this prep.

It wasn't just classical music and opera around the house. My father adored Gilbert & Sullivan, Stephen Sondheim, and others.

There's a home video of me at six years old holding the record *A Little Night Music* and singing along with it. Six years later, my father became one of the early investors in Sondheim's *Sweeney Todd*. He fell completely in love with the music and libretto, macabre as they were. Before we went, he and I sat on the couch and read the libretto together. Then he took me to the preview performance on Broadway, which was thrilling. We laughed a lot at the puns in "A Little Priest," and to this day, *Sweeney* is one of my favorite pieces.

It's interesting how so many memories of my father have to do with music. Once in Aspen, we were out to dinner with friends – a woman and her three children (ages 14 to 21). After dinner, we piled into my father's car and drove them home with the radio playing a Mahler symphony. We arrived at their house just before it ended, and instead of just saying "good-bye" he suggested everyone stay in the car until the symphony was over, another fifteen minutes or so. Of course, he raised the volume quite high, and the sound system in the car was really great. I don't know if the other kids had ever listened to a symphony before. I think it blew their minds. They respected his passion for the music, and recognized his desire to share this with them – so we all sat quietly in the dark until the symphony was over. I believed my father wanted them to feel what he felt. And I think they did. I had the impression that my father changed their lives a little bit.

I've talked a lot about my father's love for music, but he was just as devoted to his work and to building his companies – and hiring great staff. In high school I worked for Gartner Group one summer. My boss was Mimi Ford, the head of Communications. Mimi was brilliant and funny, thoughtful and kind. She was a great listener and urged me to write poetry every week. One day she needed a favor and entrusted me with driving her stick-shift pick-up truck. As a teen-ager, I was in awe of this independent and exciting woman who my dad had hired, and who happened to be my boss.

As a kid, I recall my father taking his work with him *everywhere*. Even on the chairlift in Vermont, with skis dangling in ten-degree weather, he'd have his papers in his lap, and his Bic multi-color pen. We used to tease him about it. This was soon after Gartner Group started up, when creating the company was a 24/7 experience. Dad hasn't changed much — my father is a born analyst, and to this day he constantly takes notes on everything, critiquing and adding his own ideas. He can't just read *The New York Times*. He underlines anything that has resonance for him, whether it's an article about the Middle East, or a review of a concert he went to (where he often disagrees with the critics).

As serious and tough as my father may be as a businessman, another quality that must have helped his success in dealing with people is his joie-de-vivre. He has a silly, mischievous side that has impressed all my friends (one, a philosophy major I went to college with, still calls him his hero.) After a particularly entertaining evening, among other antics, my father poured wine into a flower and drank out of it. He's amazing at entertaining my daughter. He'll put on three hats and act as if it's normal and see if Clementine notices. Or he'll pretend he doesn't see her. She's constantly cracking up when she's with him, and he's very lovable.

My father is incredibly detail-oriented. Growing up we used to take vacations and travel mostly by car. He frequently stopped the car so we could get out and admire the view. As a kid, that quickly became tiring, but there was his expectation that we must respect the beauty of the land, that we should note the contrast of the mountains with the sky, the colors of the sunset. Now I find I do that with my daughter, and I hear myself sometimes sounding just like my father: "Clementine, look at the view." I'm pleasantly surprised to see that she has a genuine interest in views – sometimes she'll even point them out to me first.

My father's exuberance for everything in life is something I'm very proud of – it's contagious and inspiring. I'm in awe of his constant curiosity, his youthful spirit, his high standards, but also his ability to feel emotion and be moved. He's a very *human* human being.

The Compulsive Perfectionist with the Big Heart

"He is always doing something new.
Gideon is unusually open-minded."

Aaron Charles Sylvan
Gideon's stepson

Gideon's success has afforded him the very rare privilege of being able to fund the launches of his own new ventures. Most aspiring entrepreneurs face a tremendous challenge in funding, but because of Gideon's success with Gartner Group, anyone in the world will take a meeting with him and regard him with great respect.

Almost all the Fortune 500 companies are customers of Gartner, so when the founder says, "I want your ear, I'm doing something new," they all listen. And the same for financiers. Being able to use his own assets and connections and credibility to launch Giga, and to explore other endeavors of his own, was something he enjoyed hugely. Someone else in his position might have rested on their laurels, but for Gideon the game is never over - there's always a new project.

Not many people know that Gideon is a compulsive perfectionist. He is not capable of reading without a pen in hand, because nearly everything gives him an opinion about how it could be improved. He is compelled to note and articulate that opinion, and his desk has mountains of papers with little squiggle marks and notes. I'd love to see his flow of commentary turned into a blog. He's so prolific, and acutely observant, I'm sure it would be popular.

This is all so deeply ingrained in him. He could be waiting in line and thinking, "people should stand along this wall instead of that wall." Or "this gadget has four buttons on it but needs a fifth." Or "they're idiots for having the concert in this hall because it has a terrible echo on one side, so I'm going to write a letter to the Chairman of the Board and tell him they should move the singers."

Gideon has a love of gadgets and consumer electronics. He is unusually open-minded about wanting to give every new technological development a chance. He prides himself on making fresh judgments on each new thing, resisting the temptation to say, "the old one was bad, so I'll ignore the new one."

His criticisms are very incisive, so you might think he wouldn't give "second chances", but at the same time he's always open-minded.

Endless re-evaluation and re-examination brought him success in his business. Those habits served him well in developing unique, high-quality, innovative products — but they make him an exasperating travel companion. There's no such thing as keeping an agenda, because he never stops changing his plans when he thinks of a better way to do something.

Music and Art are his main passions and where he directs his charitable contributions. Some people will look at the chart of what you get for being a patron – this invitation to that dinner, how many free tickets, and so forth – and will choose how much to give depending on the benefits they want. But Gideon prefers to find organizations where he gets a voice along with his contribution. He wants to have his opinions listened to and to influence the decisions made by the organization.

If Gideon catches a scent of anti-Israeli sentiment, he will threaten to cancel his sponsorship and he will follow through. I believe he just did that with a noted music school. It ran an editorial in its newsletter that made him furious. While he is generous with his fortune, he will always vote with his wallet when it comes to Israel.

Gideon became an entrepreneur after the age of 40, and then went on to build a world-famous brand, start and exit multiple successful startups, and earn millions for himself as well as hundreds of other people. Would he have guessed this from his start in Brooklyn, or his tough times at MIT? Probably not, but he should serve as an inspiration to all who believe that it's never too late to earn a great payoff — if you *work hard, persevere, and seize opportunities* that present themselves (even if they're unexpected ones). Imagine how different this story might have been, if Gideon hadn't accepted Neill Brownstein's suggestion to start Gartner Group?"

A Man Who Thinks Big

"Gideon expects not only outward elegance but
intellectual excellence and clarity of thought."

Rabbi Brad Hirschfield
President, CLAL – The National Jewish Center for Learning and Leadership

Gideon and I first met about fifteen years ago in Aspen, where I was speaking at an event at the St. Regis. This hyperkinetic, rail-thin, white-haired guy wearing bright red-framed glasses came up to me and started firing questions at me. He had questions about Israel, and Judaism, and my life story, and the meaning of life. I was answering just as quickly, and we just had at it. It was like going into a batting cage where the machine is set at "fast pitch" and you're just cranking to keep up.

After about 45 minutes, I looked at him and said, "Who are you?" And he finally introduced himself. Truthfully, I didn't recognize the name Gideon Gartner, but I realized in the course of that first meeting that I had met someone who really thought big. And for all of the time I've since known him, that is one of the defining features of who Gideon is, not just in the world, but as a friend and even as a mentor.

Our friendship developed from that afternoon. For the first couple of years, it was just a summer friendship. I spend a chunk of each summer teaching in Aspen, and Gideon was out there for the Music Festival. We enjoyed talking about everything from emerging trends in communication, to the state of the world. I have no business background and Gideon has a limited background in Jewish stuff, but we both understood that the facilitation of human knowledge is crucial to the advancement of the human condition.

One of the things Gideon taught me is to trust thinking really big and not to worry about the lack of immediate answers. That was something I believed in because it's part and parcel of my approach to human growth and spirituality. But for someone to be so rooted in that approach in the business world, where it's testable and measurable and profit/loss-able on a minute-to-minute basis, was really interesting.

One of the motifs of our friendship is that Gideon comes up to me at critical moments and, out of the blue, fires off an important question. A few years into our friendship, Gideon said to me, "Why aren't you writing more?" I hadn't written any books at that time. It didn't dawn on me that taking writing seriously was something I was going to do or even thought I could do. I said, "I'm really a talker, not a writer." He said, "That's not acceptable." I asked, "What do you mean?" He said, "I want to tell you something. You don't have to write anything big. You could write a couple of sentences every day. But when you answer questions, you should share them with people."

His point was that you shouldn't wait for something to be finished in order to share it because everything in life is ongoing revision. He said, "When I was at E.F. Hutton, every morning I would write several sentences relating to investments and send them out to all the sales people. Some of them were gems, although the truth is, many of my comments probably weren't all good. But just the fact that I did it made a difference."

I was really moved by it although it didn't change anything for me for a year or two. But during that time, we were starting to get together more in the city, and he would always ask me, "Why aren't you writing?" So when some opportunities for writing came along, I could have pushed them aside. But his insight that I need not worry about producing a perfect finished product is what allowed me to accept my first regular writing commitment as the first Jewish blogger for *BeliefNet.com*. That led to my writing for the *Washington Post* and writing a couple of books.

In many ways, that was because of Gideon. His persistence, his insistence on never letting my concern with the short-term answer get in the way of thinking big – that was absolutely crucial.

Gideon has a remarkably acute sense of beauty. And in addition to beauty, of style. Style is a way of being in this world, whether it's in the music that he treasures or the architecture of Tel Aviv, about which he can wax poetic, or the way he looks at Sarah and absolutely delights in her. I was proud to marry two people so in love. Even now, he'll turn to me and say, "Isn't she beautiful?" It's not a performance; there's no one else there. And she doesn't always hear it, so it's not for her benefit. He just delights in her. He's really committed to elegance, not in the fashion sense but in the way that scientists use it.

The pursuit of elegance and excellence are what animates him. That kind of relentlessness makes him tough on himself – and can make him tough on others. Gideon expects not only outward elegance but intellectual excellence and clarity of thought. He's always up for a fight if he disagrees with your definition of "smart." But he'd rather have a good fight about what defines smart than dumb agreement.

Intellectual wrangles form the substance of our relationship. We could just turn on the news and it would be enough to set him off. But they're not fights. He sees every event as an opportunity to refine one's thinking, and he's both deeply curious and completely opinionated. So he'll say, "What do you think about this event going on in Israel?" I'll tell him what I think, and he'll say, "No, that's just wrong," and then ask me six more questions about why I think why I think.

Gideon feels deep responsibility towards his family and believes that with increasing wealth comes increasing responsibility toward those he loves. There's almost never a time when we're not together that he doesn't talk about his children and grandchild. He's not just showing me pictures of them but wondering about the substance of their lives: Are they pursuing paths that will lead to their happiness and fulfillment? Has he done the things he can do best to help them achieve those things? That stuff matters to him, a lot.

What many people don't know about Gideon is how tender he is towards those he loves. Gideon and Sarah have been at all three of my daughters' bat mitzvahs. At each one, he would find each girl at the end of the ceremony and would come up to her. Because he's Gideon, he would talk to her as he would talk to another adult, but with a tenderness that really is quite remarkable but is as much a part of him as anything else. I remember standing off to the side and watching his eyes as he watched the girls, and just being blown away.

If Gideon were a character out of the Old Testament, he would be three characters. The first character is God. Gideon delights in being larger than life and while he doesn't think that he's God, there's a sense of grandeur that he both appreciates and tries to fill up. Certainly when he thinks about business, he's a Moses. He has a sense of purpose and mission. He may not always like the people he's leading, but he's going to take them somewhere better—and we're going to get there. And there's a Job quality. He wrestles a lot with why certain things have happened, with the whirlwind that life can feel like. The idea that certain questions are unanswerable can be very painful for him.

Going Forward

Through his friendships and philanthropic activities, Gideon has greatly enhanced many people's lives. We await those contributions that Gideon will continue to make to the causes and people he cherishes.

www.ingramcontent.com/pod-product-compliance
Lightning Source LLC
Chambersburg PA
CBHW071406050326
40689CB00010B/1771